MOVING MOUNTAINS EVERY DAY

Lessons for Business Leaders in Creativity and Innovation

DANIEL STEININGER JD

MOVING MOUNTAINS EVERY DAY
LESSONS FOR BUSINESS LEADERS IN
CREATIVITY AND INNOVATION

iUniverse books may be ordered through booksellers or by contacting:

iUniverse
1663 Liberty Drive
Bloomington, IN 47403
www.iuniverse.com
1-800-Authors (1-800-288-4677)

Because of the dynamic nature of the Internet, any web addresses or links contained in this book may have changed since publication and may no longer be valid. The views expressed in this work are solely those of the author and do not necessarily reflect the views of the publisher, and the publisher hereby disclaims any responsibility for them.

Any people depicted in stock imagery provided by Getty Images are models, and such images are being used for illustrative purposes only. Certain stock imagery © Getty Images.

ISBN: 978-1-5320-6140-0 (sc)
ISBN: 978-1-5320-6139-4 (e)

Library of Congress Control Number: 2018913064

Print information available on the last page.

iUniverse rev. date: 02/05/2019

"To my father Walter Steininger and my grandfather Daniel Hoan, Mayor of Milwaukee who by their example taught me how to live a creative life".

CONTENTS

INTRODUCTION

Anyone who has faced a mountain while hiking knows there are multiple ways to handle this major obstacle. The hiker can attempt to go straight up and over; find a hiking path that has sufficient switchbacks to make the hike easier; or simply find the pass around the mountain. In Montana, where I spent a good part of my summers in my youth, there's a famous pass called Marias pass. It was used by early pioneers to skirt the daunting mountains of Glacier National Park.

Every year I now return to Glacier Park and it was there that I decided I needed to write a book about creativity and innovation. Why? Because mountains represent obstacles that either stymie or block the hiker until he or she learns how to eliminate the barrier.

All business leaders, no matter what the size of the company, run into obstacles, what I call mountains, every day that block progress. We now live in a world of constantly emerging disruptive technology so the pace of new obstacles and competitive threats continues to accelerate.

This book is intended to give any business leader the tools of creativity to be used in their personal life, and the tools of innovation in their corporate life so they can navigate the never ending obstacles to running a successful business.

My personal journey on creativity began in 1968. Our country was in the middle of a very unpopular war in Vietnam. I, like many other young men my age, was subject to the draft as America did not have an all-volunteer army at the time.

It was hard for me to imagine serving in a more unpopular war for a cause my generation simply could not accept.

What to do? I knew the problem; but I did know the solution. The Army classified me A1.

In attempting to answer that question I needed to be very creative as my life could well depend upon it.

I began by putting multiple options in play; applied to the Peace Corps, Vista (Now Volunteers of America), the National Guard etc. I was accepted to all the programs I applied for.

That allowed me to choose the best option which happened to become a teacher in Kenya East Africa as part of the US Peace Corps. My two years in Africa changed my perception of the world and my life forever.

Fast-forward to 10 years later when I was a practicing attorney in Milwaukee Wisconsin; having graduated from Boston University, one of the best law schools in the country.

One of my clients was a large insurance company that had major management problems. As their lawyer I drafted many of the contracts and got to know many of the people in top management.

When the CEO departed the board was looking for a replacement. I had a lot of friends at the Harvard Business School but I never dreamed of running a business and had no background to do it.

Yet the board kept pursuing me to give serious consideration to their offer. Now what?

Should I take on an opportunity to become the CEO of a company with no experience especially when it would require turnaround management skills?

I reached out to lawyers far smarter and older than I was for advice; and ultimately came to the conclusion that the only way I would know is to give it a test run.

I spent over a year navigating between my law practices and running an insurance company. You might consider this the "lean methodology" of testing of creative ideas.

After one year the partners in my law firm forced a decision because they did not want the liability of having an active CEO in the legal partnership.

I opted to become the CEO of the company and that decision put me on a path that changed my life forever and opened opportunities that never would've occurred or presented themselves to me had I remained a practicing lawyer.

When I became the CEO of an insurance company, and then President of the Board of Harbor Commissioners that oversees the Port of Milwaukee, I realized that both the company and the municipal port had major challenges and headwinds. The problems were pretty obvious: lack of growth; no clear vision and operational problems.

How was I going to solve those with no background as an insurance executive or maritime captain?

Then it hit me: I needed to learn how to come up with creative solutions to those challenges. If I could figure that out I could hardwire the process of creativity into the organizations I led.

So I did my homework and located a resource with expertise in teaching creativity. He was Bryan Mattimore author of the book: *99% Inspiration.*

He had advised companies like Pepsi, Kraft, AT&T and even the United States government. He became my mentor and a great resource to the top management team of the company. It eventually led to the innovation of new products including a mutual fund which garnered a national reputation.

I learned firsthand that creativity can be learned. You don't have to be born creative.

What I have learned is that there are basic tools that can help individuals lead a creative life, and companies drive innovation in the marketplace.

I used those tools and that knowledge in my role as chairman of the Board of Harbor Commissioners overseeing the Port of Milwaukee. It became the fastest-growing port on the Great Lakes winning multiple Seaway Builder awards.

You too can be creative and the real secret is that it will not only help you take on and conquer the challenges that life throws at you but it will also add a dimension of true joy to your life.

What do I mean by that?

Professor Mihaly Csikszentmihalyi the chairman of the Department of Psychology at the University Of Chicago in his book: *Creativity* describes what he calls the state of FLOW. This is the state of actual euphoria that anyone experiences when they have a creative breakthrough.

I learned from the great Dr. Edwards Deming that creativity is actually naturally in all of us. Think about it.

We learn to walk and eventually talk, one of the most complex achievements possible, by the time we are five years of age. We did it without being bribed or threatened. We did it because we wanted to achieve mastery of our environment.

You too can take that creative journey in your personal life and thereby benefit continually throughout your life by creative breakthroughs and achieve the state of Flow.

This book will give you the basic tools and most importantly give you examples of business leaders who have successfully led their companies to creative breakthroughs that helped drive innovation and success in their product or services.

This book teaches by examples, as there is no one formula that fits everybody.

This journey in creativity can also save your life. Here's a very gripping but true story.

A young Wisconsin boy Nic Volker experienced searing pain that signaled a new and unknown disease to doctors. Every possible cure for Nic had been tried. His doctors were stumped.

His mother would not give up and her persistence inspired doctors and researchers at the Children's Hospital and Medical College of Wisconsin to try a new radical plan that had never been performed before. It required the completion of human genome sequencing to discover the cause of his illness and eventually provide a cure by intervention in his defective gene.

That breakthrough historic discovery not only saved Nick's life but created a path that allows doctors all over the world to find discover and cure genetic defects in young children.

The story of creativity and innovation led the authors of the book *One in a Billion* by Mark Johnson and Kathleen Gallagher to be awarded a Pulitzer Prize.

It is a story that tells us that creativity can be the difference between life and death.

The same could be said of any company or organization.

In a post golf lunch with the captains of industry I was introduced to the former senior executive VP of Kodak. I couldn't resist asking him why none of us can ever have a "Kodak moment" anymore. What happened that a great iconic American brand disappeared from the landscape?

He told me in the late 1980s a meeting had been called by the CEO of Kodak. The focus was going to be digital photography the coming disruptive technology to the photography industry.

Kodak held numerous patents on digital photography so it was well-positioned to be the leader of this revolutionary approach to photography.

He had invited a young team working on digital photography to make the presentation to senior management that day.

Five minutes into the presentation by the young team the CEO slammed his hand on the table and said and I quote:

"Young man we are a chemical processing company; we will never do digital. Get the hell out of here!"

With that decision over 145,000 employees of Kodak eventually lost their job.

These stories demonstrate a fundamental fact about creativity and innovation; that creativity can either make or break someone's life or the life of a company.

I have led companies both private and public and a governmental agency and more often than not it was the ability of my organizations to drive toward creative and innovative solutions that determined success.

That in turn led me to start writing a column for the *Biz Times* more than a decade ago entitled: *Innovate or Die.*

There was nothing unique about that as the phrase was probably coined by Clayton Christensen of the Harvard Business School who has been a forceful voice in the importance of innovation and creativity to the life and growth of any company.

This book is not intended to be a self-help manual or an attempt to preach the gospel of creativity or innovation.

Rather it's about giving the reader the opportunity to access of the most creative and innovative practices of successful individuals or companies that have pursued that talent to their benefit and growth.

The reason I have chosen case studies is because that was my training as a lawyer when I was a student at Boston University School of Law. I also had friends at the Harvard

Business School and attended some of their classes. Both institutions use the case method as the best way to learn the law and business.

You just pick the chapter that applies to your current situation and there are stories of leaders who have successfully accomplished innovation within their organization and how they did it.

I've also included an introductory section on how to be personally creative.

Employers claim they want to lead an innovative company and they ask employees to think "outside of the box".

But how is that possible if individuals are not creative in their own personal life?

So this book divides itself into multiple sections starting with one focused on personal creativity; and the others focused on creativity and innovation in business; tools of creativity; and then a section devoted completely to case studies of individuals and companies that demonstrate high creativity and innovation.

So enjoy the opportunity to see how others have done it and figure out how you can best apply the lessons they teach from their successful creative and innovative lives.

And I'd like to begin with our own Republic the United States of America. Our "experiment" in democratic self-government has become the gold standard for implementing democratic values for all people. The very founding fathers of this country confronted the leadership of England that was primarily responsible for the founding of our country. It was led by a king and they forged a new government where the of the power would not be inherited titles but power derived from the people; that took imagination creativity and courage.

The pilgrims played a pivotal role in the new world in forging a government compact that inspired the founders of our Republic in 1776. Think about how creative they had to be to create self-government with virtually no model to follow anywhere in history!

Just as importantly creativity and new technology has been solving the world's problems for several hundred years. The list is almost endless from polio vaccine, to electric light bulbs, to steam engines computer technology in jet engines. The problems addressed by those innovative products were considered almost impossible to solve and yet ingenuity eliminated these seemingly intractable problems.

Having managed people in both the public and private sector all my life I've come to recognize that there are inflection points in everybody's life and in the life of a company or organization where it is critical make to a creative decision. Many of those decisions can be life altering and even spell the difference between life and death itself.

We are all bound by habits that are very hard to break; but the creative process requires a willingness to break habits and do things we are not particularly used to doing.

How can that happen? That's what this book is all about.

This then can become a great resource to the daily challenges that life brings us both on a personal and on a corporate level.

I'm on a mission to make sure the readers have the opportunity to live a creative life like the one that has been so rewarding to me and many of the people that I've hired over a lifetime.

Daniel Steininger JD

Section 1

Personal Creativity

As we go through the journey of life we are constantly faced with choices and decisions that will determine our future. In the deepest sense we are all creatures of what Charles Darwin called the "survival of the fittest".

"It is not the strongest of the species or the most intelligent that survive, but the most adaptable".

If you're reading this book it is because we all had ancestors who chose creative ways of adapting to the challenges of their environment and fellow humans or none of us would be here.

The world we live is now changing so rapidly that industries we have known are disappearing overnight. Some are being eliminated because of Amazon. Technology is revolutionizing the way we function and act every day.

Ask any group of people whether 20 years ago they could do an email, text, engage on Facebook or check their newsfeeds? It was not possible.

How then can we grow and prosper in a world that is changing so rapidly?

The answer is developing the skills of creativity to guide both your personal life, and as an employee of a company or organization.

It's hard to believe but creativity can be taught. We all know that Steve Jobs is a genius as was Thomas Edison. If you're of that caliber you will not need to read this book!

But for the rest of us lesser mortals we can develop the basic skills of creativity that not only enhance our chances of survival would guarantee we will grow and prosper in the process of this journey called life.

Linda Menck teaches a class on creativity at Marquette University in Milwaukee Wisconsin. She consistently asks her students who among them considers themselves creative?

Surprisingly very few ever feel they are creative as an individual.

This echoes my experience when I ask the audiences I speak to whether they their friends or relatives would describe them as creative? Only a few hands ever go up. It's heartbreaking.

This chapter is meant to inspire you to become a creative and start to take steps in the right direction.

Each chapter will help you wrestle with the basic questions of creativity and how you can go about becoming a truly creative person.

CHAPTER 1

THE IMPORTANCE OF CREATIVITY IN YOUR LIFE

If you're reading this book you have an ancestor who did the right things to ensure their survival and thereby enhance your survival. This column explores the importance of creativity and innovation in our personal lives as Homo Sapiens.

Challenge yourself to keep moving forward

Do we really need to be creative and innovative to live longer? Can a company survive without continual innovation?

Let's face it. If your ancestors had not been innovative and emerged from the survival wars of our species you would not be reading this column.

So let's look at our species. According to Heather Pringle, a science writer and contributing editor to Archaeology magazine, the accepted wisdom was that "starting about 40,000 years ago Homo Sapiens embarked on what seemed like a sudden and wondrous invention spree in Europe fashioning shell-bead necklaces, adorning cave walls with elegant paintings of Ice Age animals, and creating new tools out of stone and bone."

However she points out that new scientific evidence now indicates that innovation did not burst onto the scene fully formed 40,000 years ago but rather gained steam over hundreds of thousands of years.

Archaeologists have been uncovering the fact that the process of tool making to control the environment goes all the way back to our next of kin the Neanderthals, who 300,000 years ago concocted a birch bark glue to fasten stone flakes to wood handles. Another site was found in South Africa where lethal tips were formed over 500,000 years ago to make spears.

What's really interesting is that as our ancestors evolved the size of their brains as cranial capacity grew from that of the size of the chimpanzee, 450 cubic centimeters; to more than double that to 930 cubic centimeters for Homo Erectus. By 100,000 years ago Homo Sapiens had a brain capacity of 1,330 cubic centimeters.

Within the brain itself new subareas underwent major reorganization allowing for horizontal spaces between neurons in the area identified for creativity. It widened allowing more room for axons and dendrites so necessary to the creative process.

Now what really gets interesting is how our brains evolved. Our evolutionary ancestors learned to store memories and then access those memories when we needed to solve a problem or challenge.

If an early human encountered sharp thorns it remembered it and then brought it to the surface in fashioning tools that could be used to kill animals.

The other skill set that humans developed was the ability to share their collective knowledge with their children.

We did this by working collaboratively in groups to share knowledge with each other. Mark Thomas of the University College London said the premise was simple: "the larger the hunter gatherer group the greater the chances are that one member will dream up an idea that could advance a technology. Groups could learn from each other far better than an isolated individual or small group."

He argues "it is not how smart you are but it's how well you are connected."

We think we are advanced because of the blogosphere and the ability for things to go viral. But 71,000 years ago cultural innovations spread like viruses wherever there were large groups of people.

The growth of cities on the large-scale provided the opportunity for humans to interact and share concepts, new blueprints and designs across the sprawling network of the World Wide Web, which has enabled innovation in every facet of human life from medical to manufacturing to space travel at a rate that continues to accelerate exponentially thus enriching our lives and offering opportunities never been known in human history.

Our life expectancy continues to grow from a measly average age of 50 a century ago, to now well into the late 70s in America. That didn't happen by accident. It happened because of innovation.

In fact, older Americans actually have an advantage if they continue to learn because they have greater memories to rely on. Barbara Strauch makes the argument in her book "The Secret life of the Grown-Up Brain." With recent advances in medical technology, such as functional magnetic resonance imaging, scientists have discovered our brains can grow new connections within our brains.

The chemistry that supports this is fascinating. The crucial white matter in our brain is made up of myelin. It's white matter that wraps around trillions of nerve fibers in our brain that allows signals to move faster and to make the connections. The buildup of myelin does not happen overnight but takes years. It's no different than muscle buildup that doesn't happen without strength training.

So how do we apply this insight to ourselves and to our workplaces?

Create an innovation bucket list that will train your brain and your employee's brains:

1. Continue to learn something new every week of your life. Doing repeated crossword puzzles will not advance the size of your brain with its ability to make connections. So fall in love with the wisdom of TED; or rent audio books from the Great Courses series; or take an online course from college. Subscribe to National Geographic and the Wilson Quarterly. Read the top 10 fiction list of the New York Times. At your company you should regularly subscribe to Entrepreneur, Wire Magazine, the Harvard Business Review or Inc. magazine. Make a habit of reading the New York Times top 10 selling business books.

2. Identify social groups that challenge you intellectually. That may mean going to a book club; doing sightseeing with educated guides or attending continuing education classes with like-minded knowledge seekers. In the work environment it means continued insistence on learning new skills and new talents for all employees.

The innovative leader continually forms cross-sectional task forces that draw on multiple skills to solve major problems. Take advantage of UWM's School of Continuing Education robust program for business leaders. I teach their course on innovation. Education is not a one-time event that happened in college it is now a lifelong experience.

Our founding fathers knew this instinctively because they made it a constitutional requirement for anyone wanting to be president to be at least 35 years of age. They looked about and concluded we can't let anyone younger than that be president!

So set a personal agenda and a corporate agenda to strengthen your brain matter. It didn't happen overnight for our ancestors so be prepared to stick with a personal and corporate innovation agenda for the long haul. If you do, you have a much better chance of living longer to apply your newfound knowledge.

CHAPTER 2

CAN YOU BE CREATIVE?

Most of us ordinary mortals think about creativity in terms the great inventors or artists of the ages from Ludwig von Beethoven to Albert Einstein to Thomas Edison. They are creative geniuses.

But they do not define creativity alone. All of us in our lives can be creative. It's a learned skill. Like everything else, it takes practice.

But as a great American statistician Dr. Edwards Deming once said: "best efforts are not enough". You have to practice the right thing.

If you wanted to play new sport such as golf or you decided to take-up playing piano there are certain basics you have to learn and practice if you are to become skillful. Becoming a creative individual is no different.

There's no magic here but there are certain recommended practices that go a long way to get you used to practicing creativity on an ongoing basis.

Our history on this planet suggests that those who are able to uncover and practice creativity as a way of life not only survived but prospered.

In this chapter I share with you some ideas that are natural to very creative people. You can start applying those lessons immediately in your personal life.

I lay out some of the basics of how to transform yourself into a creative individual by giving you some ideas and tools to practice. These are things you can start to practice in your daily life. Use the four step process I have outlined in this column to plan something as simple as a vacation. You will love the results. Practice the tools outlined on small things and then expand it to the big decisions of life. It will slowly transform you into a "creative person" and you can enjoy the thrill inherent in all of us to enjoy and love creativity. Start now and you can begin the process of transforming yourself to being a creative individual.

Are you creative?

Ask the average person whether she is creative. She will tell you that she's not an Einstein, a Mozart or an Edison. A recent IBM study found that virtually all CEOs identified innovation and creativity as the most important source of revenue for their companies. But they then rated their companies, at best, 5 on a 10-point scale. If you're not personally creative, how you can be creative as a business leader? What most people don't seem to recognize is that without creativity, they would be doomed to a life of misery. Early human beings had to learn to fashion tools to defend themselves against predators, access food from the natural environment and create dwellings to live in. Over time, agriculture evolved as humans learned techniques to reproduce food.

Observe children at play. If they are not playing video games, they can create amazing solutions for building forts out of cardboard or using crayons to draw unusual pictures expressing their "inner artists." Just as instructive is the fact that creative geniuses tell us that their ability to be creative is dependent upon tremendous persistence. Thomas Edison experimented with literally hundreds of potential fi laments to find the right combination for a light bulb. Mozart put in ungodly numbers of hours working to improve his compositions for his greatest musical productions. We cannot resist the conclusion that creativity is a learned skill.

This is best captured in a great book on creativity, "99% Inspiration" by Bryan Mattimore, president of the Mattimore Group, an innovation consulting company in Stamford, Conn. In order to bring creativity to your workplace, you need to be systematic and disciplined. There are basic tools of creativity that ensure a culture that looks to solve its daily challenges with creative solutions. What is so important about having a culture of creativity is that it provides systematic approaches to solving not only new product development, but also budget problems, human resources problems, new approaches to supply chains, and the list goes on. Yes, even accountants and actuaries can and should be using the tools of creativity. In the middle of the last century, J.P. Guilford, then the president of the American Psychological Association, challenged his colleagues to change the appalling state of creative research. Thus was born the creative movement resulting in its lofty position as the No. 1 challenge for 21st Century psychologists. So what are some of the basics of the creative process that, if put in place, will create a culture of creativity in your organization? It requires adopting an approach dramatically different from the standard American thinking. Harry Quadracci, the CEO and founder of Quad/Graphics, said it best about Americans: "We...shoot, ready, aim." You are forewarned that this journey will buck the prevailing tendency of your workforce to go right to the solution for the challenges and problems facing your organization. You're also cautioned that it will take more time. But the good news is slowly but surely, you will transition to an organization that is both innovative and remarkable in its ability to solve its ongoing challenges. This is a brief summary of the basics that you can apply not only to the organization, but also to your personal life. Practice with your family and you'll be amazed at the results.

1. Define and clarify the problem

This step requires great patience, which is a real challenge in today's busywork world. Getting people to agree on the actual problem being solved is not as easy as it seems. There are multiple tools that help facilitate those discussions. Once the problem is clarified, it must be turned into a challenge statement.

2. Ideation and divergent thinking

Create multiple scenarios and multiple ideas and capture them without comment on their feasibility or workability. Ernest Hemingway came up with more than 100 titles to his novel "Farewell to Arms" before he selected the title. Consider a metaphor used by Prof. Gerard Puccio, who teaches creativity: Imagine you're in a car with your foot on the accelerator. During the ideation session your foot should stay on the accelerator and not brake. Any employee or associate who talks about why something won't work is ruled out of order.

3. Divergent thinking and evaluation

Look at the list that has been developed and begin to rank the ideas. Develop a set of criteria by which ideas will be judged. Green check those that are easy to implement; blue check those that will take additional reflection and thought. You now have a list to choose from.

4. Implementation

As you flowchart and develop the process for implementing your ideas, do not hesitate to use the other three steps to select the best form of implementation. Practice these in your personal life.If your family wants to go on a vacation, or you're going to host a party, put all four steps in place before you make the final decisions. You will find that people will have a lot more fun and enjoy the process and expand their horizons to ideas that they would never have thought of otherwise. Remember the creative process is natural and is part of the human existence. You cannot lead a creative work environment if you are not willing to practice it in your personal life. I even recommend using this to improve your golf game or develop a new musical talent. The world of creativity awaits you if you're willing to be systematic and learn new skills.

THE IMPORTANCE OF SOLITUDE

All of us have very active brains. Our frontal cortex has an executive component that directs our activities throughout the day to ensure survival. There are incoming messages from our environment that are continually being received that requires reaction on our part. How do we manage that incoming to carve out time for creativity?

That requires practice. This column outlines ways you can set aside time for "solitude" and quiet. That forces the executive component of our brains to go on hold and allow for true creativity to arise. How many people have said their best ideas come to them in the shower? Steve Jobs was famous for taking walks to stimulate his creative thinking. You need to find out what works best for you.

These columns outline ideas for you to practice and try.

Solitude

Take time to think by yourself

Please look at the graph that accompanies this column. This is the rate of technological change in our economy today. This is enough to make a normal leader turn paranoid. Steve Jobs said, "The only way we can deal with this mess is to innovate our way out of it." So how do you ensure that your organization is adaptive and creative? To begin, ask yourself: How do you spend your time at work? Chances are you spend a lot of time in meetings. The Harvard Business School and the London School of Economics burrowed into the daily schedules of more than 500 CEOs around the world. A good part of their days were spent in meetings that they had a hard time defending. Everyone preaches the value of teamwork and collaboration. Seems like a no brainer to argue that meetings are a healthy way to accomplish this.

Guess what? Many of the greatest ideas originated from thinking done when completely alone. Jonah Lehrer, writing in the January issue of the New Yorker, documented a devastating experience in the 1950s. It was conducted at BBDO. It found that when test subjects tried to solve a complex puzzle, they actually came up with twice as many ideas working alone as they did working in a group. Numerous studies have since verified that finding: putting people into big groups doesn't actually increase the flow of ideas. Group dynamics themselves, rather than overt criticism, worked to stifle each person's potential.

Susan Cain tackles this very problem in her book, *"Quiet: The Power of Introverts in the World That Can't Stop Talking."* She explained to *The New York Times* the reason why. People in groups tend to sit back and let others do the work. They instinctively mimic others opinions and lose sight of their own, and they often succumb to peer pressure. The Emory University neuroscientist Gregory Berns found that when we take a stance different from the groups, we activate the amygdala, a small organ in the brain associated with the fear of rejection. Professor Berns calls this "the pain of independence." How often have you heard people say that the best ideas come to them in the shower? Recently, I toured the SUNY Biomedical Tech Center in Brooklyn, N.Y. In the boardroom on display were the notes of Dr. Robert F. Furchgott, an extraordinary scientist who made major contributions to our understanding of cardiovascular physiology and pharmacology. He was awarded the 1998 Nobel Prize in Medicine and Physiology for identifying the fundamental role that nitric oxide (NO) plays in the regulation of cardiovascular function. He did it all by himself and his notes reflect that. Steve Jobs spent a lot of time biking through Europe after being terminated by Apple computer. It was there that he thought through the next generation of software for computers that serves as the framework for a lot of the technology of PCs today. How often have you ever seen a picture of Albert Einstein with a group of people doing research?

Here's some suggestions on how you and your staff can spend time alone thinking about creative solutions:

1. Carve out part of your time every day to sit quietly and think. It's often said that it's not unusual to see the CEO of a Japanese company sitting in his chair

staring at the ceiling. They drove our auto industry into bankruptcy. There's a lesson there.

2. Set aside reading time for books and periodicals relevant to your industry, and then take the time to reflect on what you've read.

3. Ensure that there are small private rooms that can be totally blocked off from noise for your employees to use for creative thinking time. Paint the walls with white board so they can draw solutions. Call these quiet rooms.

4. Take a walk with a CD and listen to audio books on economic trends and the stories of successful companies who compete with you. Turn it off occasionally and think about what you heard.

5. Between staff meetings assign think work to everyone and ask them to come back to the meeting with their own ideas.

6. Lastly, I'm not suggesting abandoning brainstorming altogether. Rather, consider spending brainstorming time looking for causes of problems. That's far more productive. The solutions are best sought in solitude.

Now go take a shower and think about all of this, and how you are going to change your practices based on what you've learned here.

Quiet time is quality time for the brain

Your brain is deaf, dumb and blind. It has no direct connection to the world. Inside of your head, it's always dark, wet and 98.6°. Because of the invention of MRI and CAT scans we now can learn more about the internal workings of the brain than ever before in human history. Scientists have learned that we can actually grow new connections, called synapses, between our brain cells. All along we thought our brain just lost cells and then we died! Now scientists have learned that thinking through intellectual challenges actually grows the brain which is part of our anthropological heritage.

Dr. Gene Cohen in his book *"The Creative Age"* points out that we cannot grow new cells. However creative thinking and new endeavors actually help grow existing brain cells larger and enhance the connections between existing cells referred to as axons and dendrites. Those connections are critical to enhancing our ability to think creatively. The bottom line: if you don't use it you will lose it scientifically. According to the recent *Harvard Business Review* article "Your Brain at Work," by Adam Waytz and Malia Mason, there is a consensus among neuroscientists that your brain is truly never at rest. They learned that we have an actual default network that continues to function even when our mind is wandering or just "zoning out." It is referred to as "task negative" because it functions even when we're not focused on a particular thought. The default network is responsible for one of the most prized abilities: transcendence. That is the capacity to envision what it's like to be in a different place, in a different time, in a different person's head or in a different world altogether. This is unique to humans. During transcendence people detach from the external environment, stop processing external stimuli and real creativity begins. This is groundbreaking stuff. The authors point out that this discovery leads to the scientific conclusion that having unfocused free time is an important, and underutilized factor, in breakthrough innovations.

We can now understand the purpose of Google's "20 percent time" policy under which company engineers get a day a week to work on whatever they want. While these programs are an excellent start, all of us agree that really detaching from the work environment is a near physical and mental impossibility. Intuitively, we often admit that some of our best ideas come when we're in the shower or out for a walk or maybe even on a golf course. Time and time again some of our best solutions have come when we've walked away from a problem. Authors who get stuck in the middle of writing a novel tell us they often "put it on the shelf" when they develop a creative block. All of this is easier to say than to actually accomplish as we compete daily to ensure the success of our businesses. But the science is no longer in dispute. Our default network is functioning and does need the right conditions to drive innovative thoughts and stimulate creative thinking. So how are you supposed to find time to isolate yourselves or our employees? You can begin by building quiet times into your own daily schedule every day. It may mean solo daily walking or sitting quietly in the dark room without interruption. It's important to you not only in your business life but in your personal life as well.

Companies should think through a strategy. Ideas could include:

»»Establish a "creativity room" which is dedicated to staff brainstorming sessions.

»»If you're a manufacturing company, you could follow the lead of the Detroit Tech shop. They established a facility stocked with laser cutters, 3D printers and CNC machine tools. Anyone with manufacturing skills could try out their ideas. Ford Motor Company is allowing some of its engineers to use the facility.

»»If you're in the software space you could do a one-day Hack-a-Thon. Define the software problem that needs to be solved and award a prize for the employee who can come up with a solution during an eight hour session.

»»Schedule downtime when employees have no electronic access to e-mails, telephones, calendars etc.

»»Send employees on missions such as visits to libraries or other sources of inspiration and require them to share the insights they come up with on their return.

»»Encourage people to sleep. You heard that right! Everyone should get their sleep. Studies show that your brain processes ideas while sleeping as well as regenerates itself. Sleeping is critical to the innovative and creative process.

There are no easy solutions and the science is relatively new. But the evidence is clear. Use your newly acquired quiet time to think through building "innovative time" into the daily schedule of your employees as well as in your own personal life. It will accelerate the new ideas and innovative thinking you and your company needs to survive and prosper.

Growth of World Population and the History of Technology

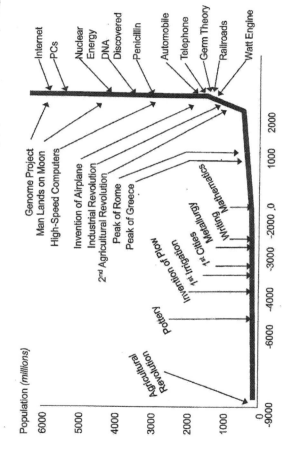

Source: Milken Institute, Robert Fogel/University of Chicago

INNOVATION
AMERICA® 2011

4

You are never too old to be creative

Everybody thinks creativity belongs to the young. Mozart was age 6 when he started composing music symphonies. Mark Zuckerberg and Bill Gates were dropouts of college at a young age and starting some of the best companies on the planet. But those are not the rule of thumb. Creativity can occur throughout our lifetimes. Col. Sanders was 65 when he launched his company Kentucky Fried Chicken.

We are never too old to be creative

We keep hearing about all the young techies creating the latest cool app for our smartphones, and we think creativity belongs to the young. History and human biology suggest just the opposite. Some of the greatest breakthroughs of the ages came from adults in their 70s and 80s. Let us not forget that Steve Jobs was beginning to hit his stride in this mid- 50s, before his untimely death. He was terminated by Apple Computer when he was younger because of his failure to grow the business. Thanks to new technology and science, we are now better able to understand how the brain functions and why older Americans have such a distinct advantage. There are two types of creativity: creativity with a big 'C,' represented by Thomas Edison and Albert Einstein; and then there's the ordinary daily activity with a small 'c,' in which we all identify problems and frustrations and come up with creative solutions to them within our personal life or business.

Historically we knew that brain cells gradually decline as we grow older. What we didn't know until the creation of MRI machines that can do CAT scans is that between our 50s and late 70s, our brains increase the length and number of cell branches, called dendrites, in different parts of the brain. Just as with our physical bodies we need strength exercises to grow muscles, our brains need mental exercises to grow these new neurons and dendrites, and that can include learning new things and not repeating what you already know. If you learn a new language, you're guaranteed to grow a lot of brain neurons and dendrites.

That gives us a unique advantage in processing information so necessary to the creative process. Over our lifetime, we collect experiences and learn from mistakes. Then we translate that information into wisdom, which allows us to increase our ability to define problems quicker and to tap our wealth of experience to identify numerous solutions to problems.

Walt Whitman captured it best in one of his poems written when he was in his 70s: *"Youth, large, lusty, loving – Youth, full of grace, force, fascination. Do you know that Old Age may come after you with equal grace, force, and fascination?"*

If you doubt me, check the ages of Nobel scientists. Or just look at history and the list of famous artists, scientists, musicians and philosophers who did their greatest work in their 60s, 70s and 80s. Some of the greatest minds of the ages prove this: Bertrand Russell, Picasso, Titian, Beethoven, George Burns, Dr. Fred Sanger, who won a noble prize in chemistry in 1958 and again in 1980, and Stanley Kunitz, who won a national award at age 94 for his book, *"Passing Through."*

There's another reason that aging drives creativity. Dr. Gene Cohen, M.D., Ph.D. author of the *Creative Age* makes a very important point. Most adults inevitably face loss and adversity that comes with the very fact of our humanity. Adversity comes in an infinite variety – illness, death of a loved one, job loss, or any undesirable change – any event or situation so negative that it causes extreme uncertainty.

Many of those life changing events produce feelings of anxiety, despair and helplessness, as well as loss of control. Creativity is a powerful antidote to adversity. Dr. Cohen makes the point that creativity is an emotional and intellectual process – a mechanism that can, moment by moment, displace negative feelings, such as anxiety and hopelessness, with positive feelings of engagement and expectation.

He gives the example of the great American artist Grandma Moses, who exemplifies the synergy of creativity, age and adversity. She spent a lifetime helping her family make ends meet. At 67 her husband died, so she developed the talent of embroidery to support herself. By age 76, arthritis prevented her from doing any more needlework. So at age 78 she took up painting instead. Her famous painting career continued to the age of 101 when she painted her last great canvas, Rainbow. Ironically, old age can produce creative breakthroughs even as it takes away other skills.

There's no way to romanticize loss and hardship. Nevertheless, there is a relationship between loss and creativity that is worth putting on everyone's radar. Wisdom comes to us largely as a product of age smarts and emotional and practical life experiences that we have all gone through. The famous Swiss psychologist Jean Piaget described this as "post-formal thought," when we integrate our life experiences and transform them into wisdom.

Fortunately, we are in a unique time in history. Because of the growth of technology, individuals have never been better positioned to expand their opportunities and drive new creative ways to solve life's problems. Science now tells us we are never too old to be creative and to innovate.

CHAPTER 5

PRACTICING CREATIVITY

Any challenge in life we take on whether it's learning a new language; new job skills; a new sport even attending cultural events all require certain basic training in the correct techniques necessary to succeed. We've all heard "practice makes perfect". Malcolm Gladwell claims that the great athletes spend at least 10,000 hours practicing the required skills to achieve success in the given sport.

Creativity is no different. It just doesn't happen. There are certain techniques that have been proven successful in training anyone to think creatively.

Please read a survey of some of those suggested techniques and then start employing them in your daily life and watch your creative IQ jump!

Top creativity techniques drive Innovation for survival

Have you ever done any rock climbing? Probably not, as you are too sane. But did you ever observe anyone doing it? Virtually every move on the face of a rock wall requires creative techniques to successfully climb that wall. Without those techniques, the climber risks serious injury or death.

Guess what? Business is no different. Every day we are climbing a wall, overcoming competition and risking the life of our companies if we fail to make the next right creative move. The great economist Joseph Schumpeter, in his classic work "The Theory of Economic Development," observed that capitalism is at its very heart and soul about "creative destruction." This means that existing companies not only face competition in their industries, but the really great companies also cannibalize their own revenue streams in order to keep up with the competition. According to John Hagel, writing for Innovation Excellence in July 2014, forces today are potentially improving technology and therefore, "offering untapped capabilities that can be a catalyst to fundamentally re-think business models and institutional arrangements."

As a result, new approaches are rendering obsolete a significant part of existing assets for incumbent businesses. This macro level force is explaining why we experience more frequent and widespread disruptions on a global scale.

He points to research in support of this argument by Richard Foster, who looked at the average lifespan of companies in the S&P 500. In 1937, at the height of the Great Depression, a company on the S&P 500 had an average lifespan of 75 years. By 2011, that lifespan had dropped to 18 years – a decline in lifespan of almost 75 percent.

At the same time that humans are signify cantly increasing their lifespans, large companies have been heading rapidly in the opposite direction.

If large companies, with all of their resources and brand power, are facing these kind of headwinds, can you imagine what it's like for the average company today? Brutal. Now more than ever, it is important to drive creativity and innovation throughout your organization to ensure survival.

Remember, creativity is something you can learn. Even the greatest geniuses may have been born with potential, but without them developing a disciplined approach to creativity and innovation, we would not know their names.

Here are some suggested creativity techniques that you can apply both in your company and in your life personally:

1. Capturing your ideas: Almost every smartphone on the planet has an application that allows you to quickly record new ideas. Capture those ideas instantly whenever they come to you, whether you're on a walk, driving a car (hopefully hands-free) or departing from the shower.

2. Sleep: According to Hannah Newman, our creative breakthroughs during waking hours must be consolidated at night. This is the process whereby we strengthen the neural connections within our brains, and more importantly, create new

connections between neurons. Just like any athlete needs time to recover after a great performance, your brain needs sleep to fire on all cylinders. The more scientists study sleep using modern technology, such as PET scans, the more they can actually validate the value of nighttime processing and synthesizing that goes on in our brains.

3. Exercise: The more we know about how the brain functions, the more we recognize that activity in our physical bodies fosters activity in our mind. A recent study from Stanford University's Graduate School of Education found just eight minutes of walking boosted creativity by 60 percent. It may be that activity improves your mood and therefore creativity comes more easily because you're feeling good.

4. Creativity room: Smart workplace design now dedicates certain conference rooms solely for creative sessions. Decorate those conference spaces with zany posters or unusual art. The environment should communicate that it's time to turn off the judgmental button in our brains and experience the joy of pure creative thinking without an immediate need to implement the ideas.

5. Let the introverts be heard: Time and time again, meetings are conducted and extroverts rule. Unfortunately, almost 50 percent of the population is introverted and they have creative ideas they are hesitant to share. You might want to establish submission of ideas by email or anonymous

suggestions so that everyone is heard in any given creativity session.

6. Plagiarize: Some of the greatest creative minds in history have adopted their ideas by observing those who have gone before. Einstein is said to have built many of his theories on the shoulders of scientists who established major breakthroughs before his time. Steve Jobs' smartphone combined the previous existing technology of cameras, cell phones and MP3 players into one device.

7. Read: Make a practice of scanning new developments in your industry or related industries. Never before has there been a greater glut of information, with new ideas percolating constantly. You don't have to read about everyone, but you should target new and disruptive ideas. TED lectures are a great place to start.

8. Practice at home: You want to take a vacation, so involve your entire family in creating multiple options and activities they might want to pursue so everyone gets in the habit of ideation. Keep your foot on the accelerator and don't break during the idea generation session.

It's important to understand that all of the above techniques are driven by the importance of divergent thinking. That means creating ideas and potential actions that can drive innovation.

Late-night comedians have their staffs submit multiple jokes or humorous scenarios before they create their final list.

Only when the divergent thinking is complete and there's an extensive list of ideas can you begin the process of selecting of the best.

By incorporating any of the above techniques on a daily basis in your personal life and in your corporate culture, you will ensure that you are doing your part to stay ahead of the inevitable march of creative destruction in our economy.

CHAPTER 6

APPLYING WHAT YOU'RE LEARNING

Now is your chance to put creativity to work in your life with a great impact on your personal well-being.

Start with a pledge to yourself to identify a habit in your life that if changed would substantially improve your daily existence. It may be simply exercising more; losing weight; watching less TV; driving more attentively without texting or looking at your cell phone. Nobody on the planet can survive without habits as they are necessary to navigate everyday life. A great book worth reading about habits is: The *Power of Habits* by Charles Duhigg

However, some of those habits can be detrimental to our health and well-being such as excessive drinking, eating, procrastination, poor driving habits etc.

Now is your chance to use the tools of creativity to change that habit. There's a great book giving the prescription to change a personal habit by a recovering alcoholic who broke his addiction. *It is: Mine Hacking: How to Change Your Mind for Good in 21 Days* by Sir John Hargrave.

He recommends begin by writing down the habit you want to break and the goal you develop that will measure success. The process of writing a goal down is critical to breaking the habit in bringing about success. John Lehrer in his book: Imagine; How Creativity Works set a very succinctly: *"until it's on paper, it's vapor"*.

Then create some reminders posted on your nightstand, screensaver, in your study or wherever that keeps that goal in front of you. He mentions how Jim Carey wrote a check to himself for $10 million when he was really poor but had aspirations of being a Hollywood star. Eventually he was able to cash that check and a lot more!

Sir John Hargrave also recommends that you visualize not the goal itself but the steps you will take to get there. For example if you're a golfer you should visualize practicing putting for maybe two hours a week; if you're on a diet you should visualize avoiding sweets every other day; if you procrastinate visualize getting something done early at least once a week.

Develop "mini-goals" to document progress and get the satisfaction and powerful way to reinforcing your progress.

Get started now on breaking a habit using the tools of creativity. That will prepare you for contributing creatively in the work environment.

SECTION 2

INNOVATION IN THE WORLD OF BUSINESS

"Even if you're on the right track, you'll get run over if you sit still".

Will Rogers

No company can survive without sales revenues. And where to sales revenues come from? One word: innovation.

If the product or service you offer is not in some way innovative and distinct in the marketplace the long-term prospects for the company are dim.

One of the reigning gurus of business was Peter Drucker has famously observed: The business enterprise has two functions: marketing and innovation; all the rest are costs".

We live in a world of disruptive technology. Thousands of bookstores are no longer in existence thanks to Amazon. Yet even Amazon started to build actual brick-and-mortar stores so there still a role for those retail establishments.

To make it in today's world the most valuable skill will be the ability of a company to be creative and innovative.

A few years ago IBM commissioned a study of 1500 CEOs from 60 countries and 33 industries who concluded that creativity is the most important leadership quality for success in business, exceeding competencies such as integrity and global thinking. The CEOs told IBM that today's business environment is volatile, uncertain and increasingly complex. Because of this, the ability to create something that's both novel and appropriate is top of the mind."

Yet most CEOs when asked to rank their own company on average a 5 on a scale of 1 to 10.

(A) The Problem:

Business will talk a great game about wanting innovation and creativity in their companies. But time and time again in working with corporations I have discovered there are inherent barriers to any individual wanting to pursue a creative solution to solving a problem.

Everyone can recognize what we hear constantly in ongoing meetings and in the hallways of any company with new ideas:

> ➢ we tried that before
> ➢ it will be too expensive

➢ it might eliminate my job
➢ I will get into trouble if I push my idea
➢ it's not in my job description
➢ there is no reward for doing creative projects outside of my expected responsibilities
➢ promotions are not necessarily tied to creative thinking

(B) The Solution for Corporate America

There is no quicker way to change a culture to that of one that is creative and innovative than studying how other companies have succeeded in achieving growth through innovation.

Therefore the balance of this section will explore and reveal the stories by individuals and companies who were able to prove what it means to be innovative and business to grow and thereby survive.

It will not preach but rather teach by telling stories in various columns I've written over the years about businesses that faced challenges in innovation and creativity.

I will share a personal war story from my days as Chairman of the Board of Harbor Commissioners that oversees the Port of Milwaukee. Milwaukee is home of an international port. It's port had struggled for years with declining tonnage and morale was at low ebb.

As chairman of the board it was my responsibility to get a better player to lead the charge of the port. Therefore I replaced the then port director Adm. Roy Hoffman with a business leader who had run his own company in Houston, Ken Szallai.

His greatest challenge was the fact that Milwaukee could not compete with the international coastal ports in the United States because the St. Lawrence Seaway was closed to all Great Lakes shipping through the winter months.

Ken had a creative solution. He petitioned the United States Coast Guard to allow barge traffic on the Great Lakes as far as Milwaukee. After introducing that barge service Milwaukee was able to utilize those barges to head down to the Chicago River then to the Mississippi and then to the port of New Orleans year-round.

That was just one of many initiatives such as creating multiple partnerships with private industry to provide major new forms of revenue from cement distribution; steel warehousing; fertilizer domes; wind energy shipments; supply in the streets of the state of Wisconsin with salt shipped in from Canada.

The result of his creative energy was to make Milwaukee one of the fastest growing port on the Great Lakes that won every Seaway Builder award for years!

It took a lot of creative thinking and real innovation to make it happen but it did. It proved to me that even the worst case scenarios can be turned around with great creative thinking.

Peter Drucker has defined the two classic types of innovation in business.

Most companies spend 90% of their efforts in incremental improvements to their existing products based on careful market research and customer needs. Most companies know their core products and spend considerable expertise and money in tweaking those products to provide new sales opportunities. All of us buy cars and we know that the newest model has features and style changes that induce us to buy those new cars.

The other form of innovation is to create new markets that revolutionize existing markets through disruptive innovation. Starbucks change the world of coffee shops; Amazon disruptive booksellers in retail markets; Facebook created a whole new way of social interaction; Steve Jobs created beautifully designed products that served consumer needs in a way it never been done before.

Today we constantly use technology that replaced what we thought was the gold standard of how we access information or perform various tasks. Just think about it?

- ➢ Cell phones have replaced land lines
- ➢ Online news as replace traditional newspapers and magazines
- ➢ Our cameras are now inside of our cell phones
- ➢ Hiring contractors can now be done by the Internet
- ➢ Grocery stores now provide ready-made meals

> ➤ Even in sports things like tennis rackets and golf clubs have changed dramatically and in the process change the face of the games
> ➤ Entertainment has moved to online streaming and mailed in DVDs

The list is endless.

There's an old phrase: "you can be either the leader of the parade or get run over by it"

Therefore this section will define chapter by chapter the best practices in both types of innovation both incremental and disruptive.

CHAPTER 1

OUR KODAK MOMENT

In the life of every business there are critical pivot points which: leaders to either adjust to changing market conditions or face extinction. In the United States, over 70,000 manufacturing plants have closed since 2000. Many were disrupted by free-trade and labor costs in other countries.

Recently manufacturing is starting to stage a comeback which seems to demonstrate that many of those businesses could have been saved.

So let's begin by pointing to an example of how any business spells its own doom by its unwillingness to adapt and change.

There's a reason we no longer have a "Kodak moment". Kodak was the predominant brand and photography so much so that it became a household word. How is it possible the company of that size with a global presence of 145,000 employees could possibly have faced extinction?

John Kotter, Professor at the Harvard Business School in his book *Leading Change* systematically documented the reason why so many companies resist the critical nature of constant innovation and change. The list is almost endless but most of us know by instinct the fact that incumbent bureaucracies of most companies don't embrace the need to change. Many companies, according to Professor Kotter, often get arrogant and insular in thinking and resist the dramatic shifts that undergo any sector of the economy in any given business.

Read and weep about the true story behind the demise of Kodak.

Not a pretty picture for Kodak

The enterprise that does not innovate, ages and declines
"Necessity Is the Mother of Taking Chances,"
— Mark Twain

We are all watching a very dramatic "Kodak moment." Eastman Kodak recently fi led for chapter 11 bankruptcy protection. Its stock now lists at less than a dollar and was delisted from the New York Stock Exchange. Employees are worried about their jobs, and suppliers are getting nervous.

How could this iconic American company be facing the possible end of its existence? At its height in 1988 Kodak had more than 140,000 workers churning out everything from cameras to motion picture film, floppy disks and pharmaceuticals. According to USA Today, it finished that year with $1.4 billion in profit.

Last year I met with a senior Kodak official, since retired, who was at an important meeting in the late 1980s. One of the young technological stars in the company was making a presentation to the CEO on digital photography. The meeting was scheduled to take two hours.

Five minutes into his presentation, the CEO slammed his hand on the table and said Kodak was a chemical processing company and would never turn its back on its known expertise. Chemical processing was its expertise. Digital would never be part of Kodak's world. The meeting ended and the young man left in humiliation.

The Japanese company Fuji film smelled blood in the water. It led the explosion in digital photography which ironically was the technology that Kodak researchers had actually invented. They left Kodak in the dust.

Now let's look at how a local, much smaller company handled a technological innovation that challenged its existence.

In Wisconsin Sonny Ahuja started a new company in the perfume business and grew it successfully with brick-and-mortar stores at Northridge, Southridge, Capitol Court, Brookfield Square, Regency Mall in Racine, East and West Towne malls in Madison and the Fox River Mall in Appleton. He was also doing trade shows across the United States.

Roughly five years ago sales started to drop significantly with the rise of Amazon, eBay and other discount sites on the Internet. Perfume can be easily bought online, although it escapes me. Why? Because you can't smell the stuff online.

But rather than put his head in the sand as Kodak did, Ahuja learned how to design e-commerce websites and launched Grandperfumes.com.

He then learned how to do search engine optimization (SEO) to attract visitors to the site, and then mastered social media so he now has 50,000 Twitter followers and 5,000 Facebook fans and friends.

"I did what I needed to do to survive," Ahuja said. Six years ago he barely checked his emails. Now he's a social media consultant and an SEO expert focused on developing revenue producing websites.

Because cash was tight during this traumatic transition, he hired his wife Ami (Mrs. Milwaukee 2011) to help manage the perfume business. Fast forward…she now runs Grand perfumes while he focuses on growing his social media business.

As business leaders, we all have choices. Peter Drucker, the dean of American management theory until his passing, captured it best when he said: "The enterprise that does not innovate, ages and declines." Truer words were never spoken.

Innovation and creativity requires learning new skills and adapting accordingly. This is never easy. If it were, success in the marketplace would be simple.

But remember this, when you use your God-given talents and intellectual horsepower to develop new skills you become a more fully developed human being. You will enjoy the pride that comes with learning new skills and developing new talents.

The CEO of Kodak refused to develop an understanding of digital technology because he was afraid to admit not knowing something. He lacked the humility of a true leader.

On the contrary, our local entrepreneur Sonny Ahuja embraced his lack of knowledge and now leverages his expertise to help others. Not only did he save his business and strengthen it, but he created a new business and another source of revenue. He was willing to take a risk.

Kodak is busy selling its assets and patents in order to survive. Sonny is busy growing his businesses that capitalizes on new technology in the marketplace. Who would you rather be?

CHAPTER 2

EVOLUTION AND BUSINESS

What most business leaders instinctively know that unless they evolve their companies they will face extinction. As human beings we all live with the thought that someday we will die. However our companies can outlive us and most often do.

Every business therefore needs to recognize its number one function to survive is to pursue relentless innovation and creativity. This was best captured in the column below

Your company must evolve, or it will become extinct

Have you seen any dinosaurs lately? They were giants that dominated the Earth. They are, of course, long gone. But oddly enough, small sea mollusks have survived for 545 million years!

The greatest insight from Charles Darwin is contrary to what we normally think. Being the strongest or the smartest is not always enough to ensure survival. Adaptability to a changing environment is required. In business that's called "innovation."

Innovation is the natural response to the challenges of nature that could do us in. In business we learn that we have to innovate and adapt or we don't survive. Steve Jobs was an innovative genius. Look at what has happened to Apple stock since he disappeared from the landscape. It is down 25 percent as it struggles to compete with Samsung's electronics and Google's Android system.

So where does that leave us lesser mortals who run companies and are not creative geniuses on Jobs' level? Are we doomed? Hardly.

Innovation can be learned even if we are not creative geniuses. Think about everything you do every day of your life. If you want to change a habit that's creating problems, what do you do? You know that change will not be easy. It requires innovation and determination.

The same holds true for our companies. Every one of our employees finds it very challenging to change from the "usual way of doing things." So there is natural resistance.

What to do? The Management Association commonly referred to as MRA, is an excellent example of a company that learned to innovate and successfully adapt to changing times.

MRA was already known for its expertise in human resources, like up-todate salary surveys, EEOC compliance, employee screening, etc. However, after listening intensely to the 4,000 businesses that they served, they recognized a need to broaden their service offerings.

New technology was engulfing us, creating increased demands and requiring

> *"It is not the strongest of the species,*
> *nor the most intelligent, that survives,*
> *but the most adaptable."*

— Charles Darwin, *On the Origin of Species*

faster speed. So Susan Fronk, president and fearless leader of the organization and who had already digested a major merger with MRA in Minnesota, decided to broaden the services offered to members.

Since MRA is determined to ensure that its member businesses can successfully compete against anyone in the world and because we live in the Age of Innovation, she opened up her CEO roundtables to help members understand the basic tools that drive innovation in any company anywhere.

In recognizing the needs of her members, Fronk also identified the necessity of giving them the tools and capability of teaching lean manufacturing, lean problem-solving and lean project management so that these core competencies are drilled down to the shop floor and into the offices of companies.

MRA introduced the principles of Leadership Excellence that encouraged leaders to self-evaluate against excellence. MRA now provides ways in which members can learn new habits to drive innovative organizations.

MRA could've been content to rest on its laurels and rely on its reputation. But it didn't. Why? Steve Jobs got so passionate and excited about what he was doing that he would tell his employees and recruits he wanted Apple Computer products to make a "dent in the universe."

All great businesses that thrive and grow begin with the passionate commitment of the leader. You have to love your product or service to death and believe it will make a "dent in the universe."

Virtually none of us has the genius of Steve Jobs. But we can decide if we have a passionate commitment and belief in the products and services we offer. Without it, employees will struggle and it will be tough to recruit talented individuals to meet the technological challenges of the competition.

If they have passionate belief in what your company is offering your customers, the customers will in turn feel they are sincerely trying to solve their problems.

Ask yourself this question: Why do we exist?

Do we sincerely believe that we can make a positive difference in people's lives? If you and your employees can't answer that question with a passionate belief, then hang it up now. I tell all entrepreneurs who come to BizStarts to let us know what the critical customer problem is that they are trying to solve because that is why their company exists.

You can't improve anything you do or break unproductive habits unless you listen patiently and take time to fully define the problem your customers face.

Generally Americans are not geared to do that. Harry Quadracci, founder and CEO of Quad/Graphics, had a great way of putting it. He said the Americans' approach to problem solving is "Shoot, Ready, Aim."

Customer-focused organizations are more willing to embrace change because they listen and passionately believe in their ability to deliver solutions to the problems they learn about from their customers. MRA chose to listen carefully to members (ready), then innovate service offerings based on what they learned (aim) and finally expand services to members (shoot). The result was success!

So when your business environment starts to change, don't go the way of the dinosaur. Learn to innovate or die!

THE HEART AND SOUL OF ALL BUSINESSES IS CREATIVITY AND INNOVATION

There are two schools of thought when it comes to innovation in business. One school of thought points to the creative geniuses who led new companies by creating new technology out of whole cloth. They did not consult consumers or do ethnographic research. They were geniuses and they sensed a need in the marketplace.

Henry Ford once observed: "if I listen to customers, I would give them a faster horse".

Thomas Edison and Steve Jobs come to mind is true creative geniuses who invented disruptive technology that change the world as we know it and created worldwide successful companies in the process.

In all instances pure creative genius and ingenuity were able to solve problems or meet challenges that change the world for the better and attracted on ending stream of customers.

Any survey of the history of ingenious inventions produces almost an endless list. In this column I captured some of the highest ranking inventions that have changed the world in a way that was not foreseeable. They are all a great testament to the inherent genius of human beings to use raw intelligence and imagination in a way not thought of possible.

Ingenuity will solve the world's problems

"The power of population is indefinitely greater than the power in the Earth to produce subsistence for man."
— Thomas Malthus

The news media reminds us almost daily of the dire predictions of thinkers like Thomas Malthus and the limitations of the Earth's resources. For example:

"One day we hear that global warming is leading to rising seas so that the coastal areas of the United States will soon be underwater.

"The next day we hear we are running out of fresh water and it will replace oil as our most limited resource.

"Then we learn that automation is replacing workers and therefore there will be no jobs.

It's enough to send us to the local bar or pray for the day marijuana is legalized in Wisconsin so we can take away the pain of knowing the end is near!

But there are voices out there arguing that our ability to innovate solutions to our problems is actually getting better, not worse.

What amazes me is that it actually took a British citizen to argue that we do have reason to be hopeful. Matt Ridley, a member of the British House of Lords, argues in his book *"The Rational Optimist"* that such pessimism cannot be justified by the actual truth of history.

Consider some of the major innovations that have dramatically changed the outcomes of our daily living and the course of our world.

The wheel: It made the transportation of goods much faster and more efficient, especially when affixed to horse drawn chariots and carts.

Tens of thousands of other inventions require wheels to function, from water wheels that power mills to gears and cogs that allowed even ancient cultures to create complex machines. A huge amount of modern technology still depends on the wheel, like centrifuges used in chemistry and medical research, electric motors and combustion engines, jet engines, power plants and countless others.

Printing press: Gutenberg combined the idea of block printing with a screw press (used for olive oil and wine production).

The printing press allowed enormous quantities of information to be recorded and spread throughout the world. Books had previously been items only the extremely rich could afford, but mass production brought the price down tremendously. The diffusion of knowledge it created gave billions of humans the education they needed to create their own inventions in the centuries since.

The light bulb: When all you had was natural light, productivity was limited to daylight hours. Light bulbs changed the world by allowing us to be active at night.

Communications: Transmitting signals wirelessly using electromagnetic waves was a concept worked on by many inventors around the world, but Guglielmo Marconi and Nikola Tesla popularized it in the early 20th century. Eventually, sound could be transmitted wirelessly, while engineers gradually perfected the transmission of images. Radio and television were new landmarks in communications because they allowed a single broadcaster to send messages to thousands or even millions of recipients as long as they were equipped with receivers.

Refrigeration: We can cool things down by taking advantage of the way substances absorb and unload heat as their pressure points and phases of matter change. The ability to keep food cold for prolonged periods (and even during shipping, once refrigerated trucks were developed) drastically changed the food production industry and the eating habits of people around the world.

Internal combustion engine: The term internal combustion engine usually refers to an engine in which combustion is intermittent. A second class of internal combustion engines use continuous combustion: gas turbines, jet engines and most rocket engines, each of which are internal combustion engines on the same principle as previously described.

Penicillin: It's one of the most famous discovery stories in history. In 1928, the Scottish scientist Alexander Fleming noticed a bacteria-filled Petri dish in his laboratory with its lid accidentally ajar. The sample had become contaminated with a mold, and everywhere the mold was, the bacteria were dead. That antibiotic mold turned out to be the fungus Penicillium, and over the next two decades, chemists purified it and developed the drug Penicillin, which fights a huge number of bacterial infections in humans without harming the humans themselves.

Contraceptives: They have drastically reduced the average number of offspring per woman in countries where they are used. With fewer mouths to feed, modern families have achieved higher standards of living and can provide better for each child.

The Internet: It really needs no introduction: The global system of interconnected computer networks known as the Internet is used by billions of people worldwide.

The computer: It's a machine that takes information in, is able to manipulate it in some way, and outputs new information. Computers are able to make complicated mathematical calculations at an incredible rate of speed. Some high performance military aircraft wouldn't be able to fly without constant computerized adjustments to flight control surfaces. Computers performed the sequencing of the human genome, let us put spacecraft into orbit, control medical testing equipment, and create the complex visual imagery used in films and video games. So relax, and the next time someone predicts a horrifying world problem I suggest you remind them that American ingenuity and entrepreneurial dynamism has always been the heart and soul of our innovation economy. We have proven we can use our ability to be creative to solve with innovation the most challenging problems of our time.

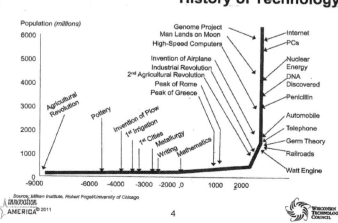

Growth of World Population and the History of Technology

CHAPTER 4

THE BLUE OCEAN

Creativity and innovation must have a target. It all begins with determining it's who will be the beneficiary of all that creative and innovative energy by your company?

If your company has not figured out the target market and the customers and is trying to attract that it cannot possibly offer innovative solutions to their challenges.

This is no easy task. So many companies fail because they choose to compete in what has been called the "red Ocean". That's a segment of the market that's highly competitive with multiple competitors forcing almost the commoditization of the product or services a company offers.

The gold standard would be to find the "blue ocean" that segment of the market that is underserved for the product or service the company will offer.

This was well articulated in the book: *Blue Ocean Strategy*; *how to create uncontested market space and make the competition irrelevant* by W Chan Kim and Renee Mauborgne. The authors also wrote a great article on it published in the Harvard Business Review in 2014: *Leading the focused organization*

In this column I outline how the process of finding your blue ocean can be gleaned by observing what others have done.

Are you swimming in the wrong ocean?

Are you in a market where the biggest players control the majority of the market and the remaining 25 percent is split between wide varieties of companies like yours?

Do you spend your time trying to figure out how to compete on price or trying to differentiate your products from the competition?

Most of us do precisely that and compete in what authors W. Chan Kim and Renee Mauborgne of Blue Ocean Strategy call a "red ocean."

As an example, in the $20 billion wine industry, the competition was fierce. Everybody in that space waged titanic battles over price, distribution, terminology, product positioning and sophistication to distinguish them from the others. They succeeded only if they could take business away from a competitor, drawing "blood" in a battle that creates a "red ocean."

Along came a new player from Australia, Casella Wines, who decided that they were going to create a "blue ocean," a new market free of competition. They found that for the mass of American adults, wine is a turnoff. It was intimidating and pretentious, and the complexity of wine tastes created flavor challenges for the average person that left him or her exhausted.

What was their solution? Target those beer and cocktail drinkers with a wine that was simple to understand. It was called Yellowtail. The wine was inexpensive and you had only two choices: Chardonnay and Shiraz (white and red).

It became the fastest-growing brand in the history of the Australian and U.S. wine industries and the number one imported wine in the United States, even surpassing France and Italy. And they did it without any promotional campaigns.

Word spread in the beer and ready to drink cocktail market that this wine was sweeter and easier to drink. It was uncomplicated and was instantly appealing to the mass of alcohol drinkers. It had upfront simple fruit flavors that appealed to this crowd. It was an easy to- drink wine.

Why did so many wine manufacturers miss the boat to a new "blue ocean"?

Steve Laughlin, cofounder and chief executive of marketing firm Laughlin Constable, has learned the answer from experience. He contends that most management teams developed the habit of cautiously extending their brands by tweaking them for incremental improvement.

A classic example is Colgate-Palmolive, which works to alter existing consumer products only slightly to improve market share. They find it difficult to develop whole new products that have not been thought of before.

So what do they do instead? How did they become the biggest name in soft soap? Simple. They surveyed the market and found that a Minnesota company invented liquid soap. The product was only marginally successful until Colgate Palmolive acquired the company and used their marketing horsepower to grow the brand.

The authors of Blue Ocean Strategy would agree with Laughlin. Too much time is focused on incremental improvement in the no-win competitive battle. Not enough time is taken to study what they call "value innovation." By that they mean exploring a value proposition that would appeal to customers and noncustomers in a different way than anything they've experienced before.

According to Laughlin, corporations are hardwired to think inside the corporate box. How do you get yourself and your management team to think outside the box?

Laughlin offers an important guide:

1. Spend upfront time to define the problem. This is very difficult for Americans to do. Harry Quadraccihad a favorite saying: "Shoot, Ready, Aim."

2. Once you have fully understood the problem and define it clearly, take a timeout. Do not look for solutions. Laughlin calls this the "incubation" period. Your brain will process all the information it has like a computer and wrap it around that problem.
3. Then one morning you wake up with the answer or emerge from a shower with some solutions. These are called epiphanies.

One thing you should consider as part of the problem definition analysis is talking to customers. Don't rely on surveys. Talk to them yourselves. See how they use your product and what they perceive to be its positives and negatives.

Do not just talk to your customers. Reach out to nonusers as Casella wines did, and see if there are markets you might be missing. Callaway Golf did the same thing when it reached out to non-golfers and found they would golf if it were made easier to hit the ball. They introduced the Big Bertha and the rest is history.

That's the essence of innovation. It requires you to get beyond your comfort zone and explore oceans were nobody has gone before.

If that doesn't work, then I suggest you buy a case of Yellowtail wine and see if it helps you in the creative process. It may not work, but at least you'll have a lot of fun!

CHAPTER 5

EMBRACE UNCERTAINTY

Embrace Uncertainty is the title of a book written by Robert DeKoch, president of the Boldt company and Prof. Philip Clampitt.

When we think about leadership of any entity the last thing that comes to mind is a leader who "embraces uncertainty". We expect our leaders to be bold insightful and people of action who can make things happen because they know what needs to be done. In the old West John Wayne represented the archetype of the strong leader who can solve problems all by himself.

The reality of business is quite different. If leaders are honest they really don't know the answers to the challenges facing their company. They need the full engagement of team members

The leader who honestly discloses to his employees that he doesn't know all the answers and he needs their help will be an immeasurably more effective leader because of the input he will then receive from his team members. It also has the advantages of hedging against overconfidence and incorporates the notion that fact-based decisions are far better off than following blindly the leaders instincts. Yes Steve Jobs was brilliant but remember he was fired because his main product lines were failing at one point in his career.

Therefore unless you are a natural born genius it's better to proceed as though you don't know all the answers if you're in a leadership capacity.

The Boldt Company

If you've ever observed the construction of a major building, you've witnessed hundreds of construction workers using a wide variety of equipment to move earth, build foundations, erect walls and transport materials.

It's hard to imagine how this all gets coordinated and that somehow the flurry of activity and noise results in a fabulous new addition to a skyline or landscape.

The construction industry has traditionally followed a top-down approach to building – an owner hires a construction manager to build an architect's plans and the construction manager hires subcontractors to complete the project along with his own staff.

The owner and builder agree to a construction management contract up front in which the general contractor agrees to a budget and a timeline.

The problem with that approach is it allows for little flexibility and adds waste to the construction process.

Just as the manufacturing industry grappled with such cost-wasting problems of excess inventory, transportation delays, unnecessary waste and defects, the construction industry has had its own efficiency problems.

In the latter half of the 20th Century, non-farm productivity more than doubled, while in the construction industry productivity fell by almost 50 percent despite advances in equipment, processes and materials.

The Boldt Co., founded in Appleton in 1889 and now one of the top builders in the nation, decided there had to be a better approach.

Starting in 1998, under the leadership of President Bob DeKoch, the company decided to practice what he eventually wrote about in his book, "Embrace Uncertainty."

Studies from Stanford University found that most construction projects resulted in 50 percent waste. That included employee downtime, transportation delays, and missteps in the design process realized when plans were executed.

It is necessary for the leader to identify a problem and reach out to others tohelp solve it. DeKoch's background was in manufacturing and he understood lean manufacturing and the benefits it brought to that sector of the economy. Boldt found 50 percent waste in construction to be intolerable.

Consequently, Boldt took the initiative, with a handful of other companies in the United States, to pioneer lean process methods in the construction industry. Boldt was a charter member of the Lean Construction Institute, formed to drive new approaches into the construction process. It has to be remembered that each building is unique, which makes construction processes more complicated than repeatable manufacturing processes.

To overcome that, Boldt introduced its Integrated Lean Project Delivery process, which now permeates everything the company does and serves to differentiate it from its peers by creating more value for its customers.

That included adopting new practices, such as better collaboration between subcontractors to identify waste, better utilization of employees, open-book accounting, reducing defects and maximizing value delivered to customers every step of the way.

The results are apparent.

The examples senior executive vice president Jim Rossmeissl points to are the highly complex Wisconsin Institutes for Medical Research tower projects at UW-Madison.

Rossmeissl said Boldt employed the Integrated Lean Project Delivery construction process, which enabled the university to make critical design changes and use funds that were saved for additions such as laboratory and research facilities – all during construction and without sacrificing timelines. This would have been impossible using the customary construction management approach.

We can all learn from the Boldt journey no matter what our business or sector of the economy:

1. Innovation and creativity are not limited to creating an iPhone or some other new device. It can also be about improving a process for delivering goods or services to customers.
2. Hire talent from other industries. They bring a different perspective to your business, as they are not bound by the habits of your industry.
3. Identify problems clearly and develop solutions unequivocally backed up by facts.
4. Embrace uncertainty in seeking solutions and be willing to look at multiple alternative approaches in resolving those problems and driving changes for the benefit of customers. Every year, step back and take the time to look hard at your business and ask your team to innovatively address the problems it discovers. This will deliver greater value to customers.

Chapter 6

Breakthroughs Require Disruption

To succeed in driving new revenues in business it is critical to offer new products and services. Some of those are incremental in nature. Many however will shake the foundations of a given sector of the economy. Amazon put multiple booksellers out of business.

But how do we do that?

It requires a culture dedicated to looking at the world from a different angle. We are all biased because of our upbringing and our perception of the world. This is particularly true in business when most people don't want to rock the boat and offend their fellow employees.

We are all creatures of habit and people get suspicious of somebody trying to change the world as we know it especially in business.

Who wants to be told they're out of line or look like the outlier?

Therefore it's critical that everybody in any as is organization understand the importance of looking at the world and your products and services from a different angle.

Here's the prescription for some steps you can take to make that a reality.

Breakthroughs require disruptions

Are you willing to challenge conventional thinking? It takes courage, and it's not easy. In his book *"Disruption,"* Jean-Marie Dru, co-founder and chairman of a Paris-based global advertising agency with offices in 27 countries, gave examples of challenging conventional thinking:

»»It was conventional thinking to consider computers as being reserved for specialists. But Apple questioned that assumption.

»»It was conventional thinking that women should grow old gracefully. But Oil of ole challenged that assumption every day.

Dru argues that disruption is about finding the strategic idea that overturns conventions in the marketplace and that makes it possible to reach a new vision or give new substance to an existing vision.

Disruption is all about displacing limits.

It is a three-step process that can be turned into a discipline:

1. Systematically identify the conventions. It's not as easy as it sounds. Our habits prevent us from identifying existing conventions.
2. Identify the problem with the convention that creates an opportunity.
3. Envision a new way of solving or removing a limitation.

Mario and Cathy Costantini decided to locate the headquarters and manufacturing plant of their now nationally famous business, La Lune Collection, in the Riverwest neighborhood of Milwaukee.

They met with police officials and found that everyone warned them that crime in the area depressed real estate prices and made it difficult to recruit talented employees.

Most of the petty crimes were caused by juveniles who had nothing to do.

They challenged conventional thinking by founding the Holton Youth Center, which provided an outlet for young people.

Their manufacturing plant is now highly successful, and is one of the reasons that Altera decided to locate its headquarters and plant only a few blocks away.

So how do you ensure that your organization systematically identifies conventional thinking and is willing to creatively look for alternatives?

Josh Linker, in his book *"Disciplined Dreaming,"* suggests a test you can administer. Take this to your team and have them answer each statement: strongly disagree, disagree, neutral, agree or strongly agree.

1. Before beginning a project that requires creativity, we always understand clearly what we're trying to accomplish.
2. We are comfortable sharing our opinions and taking risks at work.
3. We have many sources of inspiration at our disposal and rarely run out of sources of creativity.
4. My colleagues have many breakthrough ideas, and we regularly challenge and question the status quo.
5. We regularly use warm-up exercises to prepare to unleash the best in creative thinking.
6. Our brainstorming sessions are frequent, fun, focused and productive.
7. We have in place a system for sorting out the best ideas from the not so good ones.
8. In our company creativity is for everyone, not just something those "art" people do.
9. When working on new ideas, we leave our normal surroundings and find a physical environment that enables our creativity.

10. When my team works together to develop new ideas, we use many different and powerful tools to uncover our best thinking.

11. Our company has a system for measuring ideas and creativity.

12. Creativity is valued, nurtured and rewarded in our organization.

13. We are willing to challenge conventional thinking. We rarely accept things as they are.

14. We have vivid imaginations and often come up with wacky ideas.

15. Once we have a good idea, we usually test it before bringing it to the world.

16. We feel comfortable taking risks and contributing our most innovative ideas with no fear of embarrassment or retribution.

17. We regularly use metaphors and analogies.

18. We generate good ideas, and there's always a clear next step for putting them into action.

If you do not score high with lots of "strongly agree" answers, you have a lot of work to do in the world of innovation and creativity. If you don't do it now, your competitors will do it for you, and the result will not be pretty.

Mario's home country was Argentina. When he was a young child, his father applied for a telephone. It took forever because the government was in charge of the allocation of phones. When he came to America, his father asked AT&T for a phone, and within one day they had a new phone system in place. Why? The private market rewards creativity, innovation and delivery of needed services.

Your bottom line: "An optimist expects his dreams to come true; a pessimist expects his nightmares to.

"It is time to start gathering your organization and collectively answering these questions. Find out whether you really do have a culture and organization geared to innovation and creativity!

CHAPTER 7

THE VOICE OF THE CUSTOMER

Once you've ascertained segment of the market that is your primary focus then the homework begins. In today's world the leadership of innovative companies focuses on ascertaining what has been called "ethnographic research" i.e. studying the behavior of their target customers to determine their challenges and frustrations. The better the understanding of the consumer behavior then the better that translates into solutions that can solve their problems and hence increase the profit and revenue of your company.

In these columns I explained this journey and give you the reader prime examples of companies who have successfully made the journey and build new products and services based upon the voice of the customer.

Keep your eyes and ears open

Virtually all innovation begins with careful observation and astute listening.

Steve Jobs noticed that while people were walking they also listened to MP3 players, called people on their cell phones, carried cameras with them and even checked out GPS in their cars.

What if something could combine all of those in one device? Thus was born the Apple iPhone.

So, what if we are not as brilliant as Steve Jobs? (Apple, and the value of its stock, has not done so well without him.)

You and your teams can be innovative by following an established process for careful listening and understanding of customers. If you capture what you learn from this process, you can translate it into innovative new products or services.

Lara Lee, vice president of the customer experience at Lowe's, developed the entire process for identifying the customer experience when she worked at Harley-Davidson Inc. in Milwaukee.

She took the time to teach that process to the staff of Biz Starts, which now teaches it to entrepreneurs to test their startup businesses.

Jenne Meyer Ph.D., director of global strategic marketing at GE Healthcare, employs the same process in identifying new markets, customer needs and growth opportunities for education services at GE Healthcare.

On a basic level, it requires you to recognize that listening is just that: a very careful process.

When a customer or a potential customer responds to questions, they do so reflecting three realities about all of us:

1. There is a basic functional need a customer wants satisfied. So when somebody wants to buy a car, they need a vehicle to transport them from one place to the other.
2. However, most people also engage on a deeper level that stems from their emotional and psychological needs. Most individuals do not buy a car simply to satisfy a functional need of transportation. Are they trying to make a statement about their lifestyle? Do they want to prove their net worth by purchasing a high-end vehicle? Do they want to prove they are "cool" by buying a sports car? Do they want to prove they are environmentally astute by buying a hybrid? Has the safety of their kids as passengers lead them to a particular vehicle choice?
3. Lastly, what values do they hold dear that drives them in their purchasing decisions? An individual who needs transportation and wants high performance and values the environment would be a likely target for a Tesla car. Someone buying a massive SUV or truck might be interested in making a statement about power.

The process of listening and identifying deeper level needs and values should be systematized and used to approach your customers or future customers. It translates into critical information that can lead to innovation.

Meyer at GE Healthcare oversees that listening process for education services. She uses it to develop educational offerings for GE's customers. On a global scale, understanding the nuance of individual needs and values is critical to success in each market that GE serves. For example, the markets in China, India and Brazil are different.

Closer to home is Fred Anderson, CEO of New Berlin-based Wenthe-Davidson Engineering Co. His company specializes in producing tubular products that protect and encapsulate electric motors, generators, diesel engines, and every other type of motor on the planet. Anderson originally approached his customer base by trying to sell them on the value and quality of the products they produce.

What he learned is that the customers had different needs from what he was selling. He discovered that each of his customers needed and valued a customized solution.

How is he going to meet that incredible need? He recognized that he had to stop telling customers what they needed and instead deliver what they wanted and valued.

As a result, he and his team went through the lean startup training so they could dramatically do one-piece flow. They instituted what the Japanese call kanban to reduce the amount of inventory.

He has great respect for his team, and he spends time out on the shop floor with them constantly improving the process so they can deliver immediately the quick turnaround and quality customized solutions their customers want.

As a result, the newfound skill has become their core competency and became a competitive advantage because no other manufacturer can meet their rapid ability to deliver quality products to specifications virtually overnight.

As Americans we tend to want to solve problems quickly. We have to break that habit if are going to successfully innovate. Few customers can easily articulate their needs, so you need to develop a mechanism of eliciting deeper level needs and values.

By listening and observing carefully your company will be able to identify the real problems your customers face – in turn positioning you to solve those problems.

That will lead to innovation that addresses a real need in your customer base and helps ensure your survival.

Understand your customers 'decision-making process

You probably wouldn't guess that someone who grew up on a rural Nebraska pig farm would be an ideal candidate to grow a major advertising fi rm. But that's how Dan Nelson, chair of Milwaukee-based marking agency Nelson Schmidt Inc. and entrepreneur extraordinaire, would describe himself. His accomplishment was taking a small ad fi rm and growing it into a major player in a highly competitive industry on a national and global scale. The traditional advertising industry was what we see on Mad Men: smart ad executives pitching clever ads to businesses. Dan Nelson had a better idea. When he was looking to grow his agency, he recognized that the world was changing and the Internet was becoming a way of life. Why not look for a competitive advantage leveraging the horsepower of this new technology? He found if he could aggregate data on why customers made purchases, the agency could use that information to laser focus how it marketed and advertised. This approach called for deep understanding and mining of customer habits to target advertising to appeal to that base.

It goes on the assumption that all customers engage in what is now called "considered purchases," or purchases of products and services that typically have high degrees of emotional risk and/or reward. With the exception of impulse purchases, most consumers actually go through a fairly complex purchasing cycle and are influenced by a variety of factors, some conscious and some unconscious. Nelson explains that in order to make real connections with consumers that influence their decisions, you have to understand who they are, what their motivations are and how they go about choosing a brand. Influencing a person to buy a pack of gum requires a vastly different marketing approach than influencing a person to buy life insurance, or a business to invest in a new payroll service, for example. These influences apply whether the seller is targeting a business or a consumer. Understanding that information is pure gold and translates into a more focused ability to appeal to the customer. What matters most is understanding the customer mindset as they take their journey toward a decision.

Driven by this insight, Nelson's team developed a more focused, considered purchase marketing approach that taps deeper into buying behavior. That, in turn, gives the agency a competitive advantage. It can point to facts that give it and its client's unique perspectives into the complexities of these customer journeys. In B2B, almost every purchase is a considered purchase because so much is riding on every decision. In many instances, individual consumers are going through the same types of thought processes in order to make certain purchases. They're taking their time. They're seeking out more information. They're doing research.

So the agency is positioned with the knowledge and capabilities necessary to eliminate traditional B2B vs. B2C restrictions and speak to the cognitive and emotional processes rather than an arbitrary categorization. They illustrate this on their website and it has value to all sellers of products or services as it tracks the customer mindset when it comes to purchasing anything meaningful on the planet. Once the seller understands the mental journey his consumer goes through on a purchase, it helps fine tune how to go about appealing to those consumers. That translates into better use of advertising and marketing dollars. Nelson Schmidt illustrates the journey right on its website and all of us can learn from it.

PURCHASE PHASE

Explore: A purchase trigger based on need or want is biased by awareness, preference, belief and trust shaped by current experience and knowledge.

CUSTOMER MINDSET

- Who can I ask?
- What do I know and think?
- What are others doing?
- What's new?

STRATEGIES & METRICS

Awareness and Perception:

- Brand & value prop (Platform)
- Paid and earned media (Impressions)
- Social media (Sentiment

It puts the consumer and her purchasing journey at the forefront before the seller's obvious pride in what he offers and what he makes. Here's what you must be able to answer if you are to successfully drive new products and services in your company:

1. Do you understand the journey your customers take before acquiring your product or service?

2. Do you understand who and what influences their behavior and their decisions?
3. Do you understand the best method to reach them with your message?

The core of innovation is to fully understand the problems of customers from their viewpoint. That leads to creative solutions, as Dan Nelson and Nelson Schmidt have demonstrated.

Converting non-customers into customers as a source of innovation

Sir Isaac Newton discovered the principle of gravity when he was hit by an apple while sitting under an apple tree. Picasso claimed his best inspiration was from other great artists.

Todd Teske, chairman, president and chief executive officer of Wauwatosa-based Briggs & Stratton Corp., says he drew some of his inspiration for innovation from a trip with his wife to buy a washer and dryer.

Your first instinct is to laugh, until you realize Teske is dead serious.

On the trip to buy a washer/dryer for what he estimated to cost about $600 total, he ended up spending $2,600 for a Whirlpool washer and dryer. He kept asking himself, 'How had that happened?' That ultimately led to a trip to Michigan to meet with the top officials from Whirlpool.

The core to Whirlpool's innovative products is what has been named ethnographic research. It may sound like something a college professor would come up with, but what it really means is sending cross-functional teams of designers, engineers and marketers out into the world to study what consumers actually do on a daily basis. They take video cameras with them to record how customers actually use their products, and they explore the values behind the customers' actions.

"Neuroscience has shown that most human decisions are largely emotional, and made within seconds. It's the post-rationalization that can take days, weeks or even months. What that means is that most people can't actually tell you why they do what they do, or what it is that they want next. It's only by closely observing them going about their daily lives, recording the struggles that they face and the dreams they're trying to achieve, that we can really understand the unmet needs that give rise to new business opportunities," said Lara Lee, senior vice president of Customer Experience Design at Lowe's Home Improvement.

The Briggs & Stratton team began shooting video of users starting a lawn mower. One video clip captured a woman screaming with joy because she started the mower on the first pull. What interested the team was the low expectation that this woman had in her ability to start the mower. It got the team thinking about innovation from the user perspective to solve problems.

That one video has inspired the engineers and marketers at Briggs to roll out innovative products that appeal to users seeking a different experience with power equipment, such as:

Quiet Power Technology. Consumers complained mowers were too noisy. The new QPT resulted in mowers that are 65 percent quieter than previous mowers.

»»Mow 'N' Stow. Homeowners complained they needed to free up garage space, so Briggs engineers designed an engine on a lawnmower that can be stowed vertically and uses 70 percent less garage space.

»»InStart. Consumers wanted an easy start for lawnmowers. Briggs helped pioneer the automotive style of simply pushing a button in not only walk behind mowers, but riding mowers as well.

»»Pressure washers. Briggs knew women represented a large percentage of its customers for pressure washers, so it made them lighter, more powerful and easier to use for men and women alike.

There are two fundamental cultural norms that underlie this approach to innovation.

1. Leadership. It starts with humility. This is counterintuitive to what most Americans think leaders are all about. CEOs are supposed to be the smartest people on the planet. But in fact, most leaders are not geniuses. Really, truly honest ones are willing to learn and listen and absorb. Teske leads by admitting he doesn't know the answers, which

speaks volumes for everyone who works at Briggs. This leads to a culture of intellectual curiosity by everyone. Great companies are laboratories of great learning that leads to more innovation.

2. Looking for new customers. Carefully observing consumer behavior can lead to the discovery of new potential customers who have different needs than current customers. This opens new market space that expands the boundary of an industry and translates into true innovation. Embrace these two cultural imperatives and your company will end up in a blue ocean, rather than competing for the same customers in the red ocean.

SECTION 3

PRACTICAL TIPS FOR FOSTERING INNOVATION IN BUSINESS

If your company is a manufacturing company then you need basic tools and equipment to run your plant. If you are a contractor you need equipment and tools to build things. If you're a software engineer you need tools to create applications and programs to achieve successful results.

If you want to be creative and innovative then you need to have certain tools in place that are employed in every meeting that requires an outcome that represents new and unusual thinking and ideas.

This section gives you the basic tools that have to be in place and employed in all meetings throughout the organization to create a culture of creativity. These tools should be involved in every decision made by management even if it is not a new product or service. It could be as simple as changing an accounting system to reduce inefficiencies.

The tools of creativity and innovation can be applied across the board to everything in your company.

This section will outline a five-step process that should be embedded within your culture and part of virtually every meeting looking for new and breakthrough ways of running your business.

Before I outline ways to implement the process I would recommend three important practices that should guide every corporate meeting having to do with creativity and innovation.

(A.) Embed these practices in your culture throughout your company:

(i) Humor is important.

As a member of Young Presidents Organization I attended a seminar conducted by a creativity Institute from Denver at a conference being held at the University of Virginia. 150 CEOs from all over the world tried to ascertain the meaning of various acronyms for almost 45 minutes. (MFL= My Fair Lady). We got it done. Then the speaker played a humorous video clip from a popular movie; less than a couple minutes.

The speaker then put up another list of acronyms and we solved it in in less than a couple of minutes. What happened?

Humor moves you from your left analytical brain into the creative side of your mind; the right brain.

You cannot have enough humor in your meetings if you expect to get creative results.

(ii) Visual Communicating

Our ancestors Homo sapiens painted pictures on the walls of caves before they could verbally communicate in writing. It's in our nature anthropologically to communicate visually. By putting things in picture form including diagrams, outlines, flowcharts or whatever it enhances the ability for everyone to visually see the content of what everyone's talking about. So buy boatloads of flipcharts, electronic whiteboards or whatever else you want to use but make them a critical part of every meeting.

(iii) Facilitation:

The team leader, which often the president of the company or a senior executive, guides most meeting toward the conclusions they usually want to see implemented. This is the worst way to conduct a meeting. Neuroscience tells us we all have a perspective on how the world operates and it colors our thinking. People in leadership roles frequently think they always know the answer. The only way to guard against this is to bring in an outside facilitator either from outside the company or from another department. That facilitator needs to be trained on how to conduct a meeting to get maximum input from everyone attending. Most importantly it prevents the senior executive in the room from dominating the outcome of the meeting.

(B.) Step-by-step innovation process

The purpose of this section is to give you the reader tips and exercises to foster creativity in the work environment. They are organized around the five step process of innovation:

1. Problem Identification
2. Ideation; otherwise known as divergent thinking
3. Criteria for Evaluation
4. Convergent thinking
5. Implementation especially using the lean testing approach

1. Problem Identification

The founder and entrepreneur of the greatest printing companies on the globe was Harry Quadracci and the company was called Quadgraphics. Harry repeatedly warned Americans about their tendency to jump to solution before they identified the problem correctly and did their homework.

He said Americans typically can be described as making decisions by: *"Shoot, Ready Aim".*

As Americans we want to get on with it and solve things as quickly as we can. Unfortunately that's exactly the opposite what's required in the creative process.

Therefore I suggest consider the following when trying to identify the real problem you're facing at your company:

Idea: Identify the brutal facts that you know better facing your company. If you're losing market share in your topline product or the industry has been disrupted by Amazon get those facts out clearly and unequivocally so everybody knows the harsh reality of what has to be solved.

Idea: Create a cause and effect diagram outlining what you think to be the problem and then the causes of it. That helps clarify the real problem.

Idea: In trying to uncover a problem gets used to asking the question why? It's been recommended that you ask **why** five different times; each time uncovering new insights to the potential problem.

Idea: Ethnographic Research requires any given product or service team to study customer behavior to ascertain where there are some trouble spots that the company could solve by better technology or newer products or services. It requires careful observation even employing video cameras to study behavior.

2. Ideation/Divergent Thinking

Historically this is known as brainstorming. In a study by the Harvard Business School it was found that the more ideas put in play the higher the quality of the final selected solutions. 20 ideas are great; 100 ideas at the top of the funnel generates results more quality ideas at the bottom of the funnel. Someone has to be appointed to write the ideas generated on flipcharts or whiteboard.

One important suggestion to generate more ideas is to ask people to come to the meeting with their ideas written down. The reason that's important is that most people can think more creatively when not forced to do it in a group setting. Some of the greatest inventions were created by people working alone in lab

The leader should then ask if the list generated triggers some additional ideas from anyone in the group; and then capture those in writing.

Remember most companies are content with incremental improvement. That is their habit and their comfort zone. Corporate habits led IBM to ignore PCs as a new product offering because they were hardwired for the big computers; and their distribution systems all supported that kind of hardware. They needed to transform the organization into an innovative one as they were failing in both categories.

3. Evaluation Matrix

This tool is highly important. It creates a scorecard for evaluating ideas. It's not rocket science and it's not scientific but it does help the group prioritize the multiple ideas they have put in play.

So select a list of the criteria by which the given idea will be judged. That can include cost, time to market, complexity of the technology, core competency to do it, upside revenue opportunities etc.

Then evaluate each idea generated by those criteria weighted with the highest number for the most important criteria. Add up the numbers and those at the top of the list will emerge.

4. Convergent Thinking

Take the survivors and greenlight some because they're quick and easy to implement; blue light some because they're going to take additional study; and then red light those that have no chance because of the complexity or cost.

5. Implementation including lean testing of ideas.

This is where the tire meets the road; where the ideas that have been put in play are actually tested.

I founded an organization called BizStarts in Milwaukee Wisconsin to foster and encourage entrepreneurship. Over the last decade of working with entrepreneurs I have observed that the successful ones were always able to identify a problem or an opportunity in the marketplace and build new technology or a new service around solving that problem.

It should be no different when trying to innovate within the halls of a company.

Business leaders could take a page out of the entrepreneur startup world. This was best characterized by Eric Lien's *"Lean Startup"* which offers up the idea of testing product or service innovation on a customer base prior to launch.

Any company should want to limit its resources on these experiments so the mantra is to "fail fast". If it's a product a 3D prototype will suffice. Test the models on customers to get the reception. Sometimes it's important just to do a video of a complex machine and how it would operate when the technology can't deliver a prototype.

It's critical to keep test ideas on key customers to get market acceptance before a company gears up for full production. They will become your true champions and advocates if you're innovation in product or service gets to market.

This chapter captures the process.

Apply the 'lean startup' model

"Necessity is the mother of invention," is an English proverb, which means necessity or difficult situations, encourage inventive solutions.

How is it possible for entrepreneurs with little in the way of resources, a small management team, very little capital for R& D, and no customers, to take on existing companies and introduce products or services that succeed in grabbing market share from those established companies?

The answer lies in the methodology followed by entrepreneurs to launch successful companies. It's called the "lean startup."

Every business on the planet has to continually introduce new products or services if it's to survive and remain competitive.

If you are an Apple Computer or Google you have the financial wherewithal to do significant customer research and market testing before launching.

But what if you don't have a great R&D budget or are not knee-deep in market research or even cash?

Then you could try to apply the lessons that apply to startup companies who are strapped for cash and introduce new products or services in the market place.

This methodology was captured by Eric Ries, a successful entrepreneur, investor, entrepreneur in residence at the Harvard Business School and author of the book, "Lean Startup." This is a process employed by BizStarts in assisting early stage entrepreneurs. The core to this approach is to reduce the upfront cost of product development in favor of immediate tests on targeted customers. In a world with 3-D printing, rapid prototyping centers such as the one at the Milwaukee School of Engineering (MSOE) and Internet tools, this becomes highly doable.

Facebook was able to validate its model by registering 150,000 users on very little cash investment. Mark Zuckerberg was able to test his social network on the students at his dorm at Harvard without a dollar of marketing or advertising having been spent.

This approach requires you to "think small." It requires you to test your product innovation or service offering on a small group of consumers. You listen to what they say. You try to determine if they will actually pay for the new product or service. You do not want suspects. You want real customers. Talk is cheap so you want to find out if you identified a real need that they would pay for.

The process starts:

BUILD..........MEASURE...........

LEARN..........PIVOT.........BUILD.......

1. Take the time to listen to customers to ascertain the market need your product or service will address. Listen carefully. What is the problem you will be solving?
2. Then build or create a minimum viable product (MVP) whether it's a crude prototype or even a video to demonstrate what it is you will do.
3. Test it on a select number of customers to determine if you identified a real need to address.
4. Listen and learn and then be willing to pivot, which means change what you offer based on what you've learned.
5. Continue small experiments to evolve your product or service to something that has market acceptance.

6. Track the metrics of each iteration. Do not just study gross sales but look at other metrics that are very critical such as renewal rates, referral rates, etc.

The underlying thinking on this is attributable to the great Dr. Edwards Deming. He lectured business leaders in Japan in the 1950s that the most important part of the production process has to be a focus on the customer.

He flipped on its head the prevailing notion that a great business idea should be launched and customers would flock to buy.

Remember how American car companies rolled out new cars every year? Their \theory was: build it and they will come. Remember the Edsel?

In the meantime, the Japanese were busy pursuing a different approach to the marketplace because they did not have the resources of the great American auto companies.

Using Dr. Deming's advice they applied a process known as genchi gembutsu, which literally means "go see for yourself."

The approach of using the MVP helps you understand what the customer wants and needs with the lowest cost investment on your company's part.

Even Mark Zukerberg made a major mistake in allowing the Beacon program to share personal information about users with marketing firms. At the same time he was not all that interested in photo sharing for Facebook. But when his staff was able to show success on a target audience, he signed on and it proved a major hit when it was finally rolled out.

You can compete head-on with entrepreneurs if you act like an entrepreneur and use the tools we teach at BizStarts.

> Execution is critical once the ideas have been identified tested and ready to go. In order to facilitate execution I recommend that a responsibility matrix be created to clearly identify who's responsible for what in implementing a new product or service.
>
> The great Dr. Edwards Deming said it best: "Divided responsibility, he is No Responsibility".
>
> That matrix should then be converted to a step-by-step process or a flowchart to track implementation.
>
> It's important to celebrate "many successes" along the road to implementation. Do not always look for a homerun before you step back and acknowledge progress.

Section 4

Best Practices in Business

"If you always do what you always did,
you will always get you always got".

Albert Einstein

The best way to learn about creativity is to study those who have gone before.

This section pinpoints all of those inflection points in any company where developing and rolling out creative and innovative approaches secured their future.

You can identify a topic that aligns with the problem you are facing or a challenge that you see and then read about how others have dealt with it.

There is no magic formula. But each of these business leaders and companies featured identified a way to be creative and innovative in their space with their particular problem.

It runs the gamut from how to deal with the challenges of a family business to how to use the Board of Directors productively.

Just select the ones that are most relevant to you and then read about the best. No use reinventing the wheel if you can follow others who have struggled with the very problems you face.

CHAPTER 1

BOARD OF DIRECTORS AS A SOURCE OF CREATIVITY

Most business leaders must deal with a Board of Directors. It's frequently referred to as a "necessary evil". Everyone puts a brave face on but who wants your management decisions continually challenged and question. More importantly a Board of Directors has the power to remove the chief executive.

However there is a way to turn this "necessary evil" into a major opportunity for contribute into the creative and innovative energy of the company.

This column captures the "secret sauce" of making full use of a Board of Directors to the advantage of management. Enjoy and then apply what you learn.

Can a board of directors help your company be innovative?

In 1985, the board of directors of Apple Computer summarily forced co-founder and Chairman Steve Jobs out of the company and sent him packing.

That brings to mind an oft-quoted piece of advice about a board of directors: "They are a lot like mushrooms; you keep them in the dark and spread manure on them."

But there's another view that a board of directors can be a great source of creative thinking as you wrestle with some of the daunting problems facing your business.

As a "recovering lawyer," I can state the legal theory behind having a board of directors is that it has a fiduciary duty to be the "conscience of the corporation."

With that said, nobody has quite figured out how that responsibility should be exercised.

Boards often are accused of acting as micromanagers in making the life of management miserable. But some have been accused of being too hands-off and overlooking egregious crimes within a corporation, such as what happened at Enron Corp.

I believe there's a happy medium in a way that can benefit your company.

The model I suggest was learned when I was a law student at Boston University. We used the case method to learn the law. I had numerous friends at the Harvard Business School, and they also used the case method to teach business.

How does this work? Here's the drill and what I call the "secret sauce" to getting maximum benefit from a board of directors:

1. Have your management team carefully define its biggest challenge or problem in advance of any given board meeting. If you don't have any problems, then you're living on another planet!

2. Once that's agreed to, create a brief describing the genesis of the problem and why it keeps you and your team up at night. It should read like a good novel, with all the ups and downs you've experienced on the issue.

3. That brief should be sent to the board several weeks in advance of a meeting.

4. In the cover email to the board, ask the directors to bring their most creative ideas to solve the problem identified in the brief.

5. At the meeting, capture their ideas and suggestions in writing on flipcharts that can be hung around the board room. One study by the Harvard Business School suggests that the more ideas listed, the better the chances of producing quality ideas at the end of the process.

6. Promise the board your team will evaluate all the ideas at future management meetings and let it know the course of action your team chooses.

7. Capture all of those ideas and bring them to a management meeting to start the process of

evaluating the ideas through the use of an evaluation matrix.

8. After that, you can start testing on a small scale some of the ideas to find out what actually works and discard those that don't. Some will be greenlighted; some will be given a blue light for more study; and some will be given a red light and are thrown out early.

9. At future board meetings, you can report back on the ideas that were adopted and the results.

The advantage of this approach is it makes maximum use of the experience of the board members, without allowing them to force management to take up a specific course of action.

Let's face it: most board members want their ideas implemented, but that can be dangerous because they don't work in the business; consequently their ability to really understand the challenges of execution and the intricacies of what you face is not easily translated into sensible advice.

So this approach has the advantage of utilizing the board's talent and brainpower, as the directors will feel valued when you get back to them on which of the ideas you chose to implement. They will love it!

They will no longer be required to sit and listen to management as it proposes resolutions for their approval. Rather, this requires the board to be actively engaged, which makes a board meeting far more lively and more interesting, and it will attract other quality directors when they hear about this approach.

This is worth a try. And if you need help in writing those briefs, feel free to reach out to me, as I did it in my youth as a lawyer.

CHAPTER 2

CREATIVITY IN THE FAMILY BUSINESS

Anyone growing up in the family business knows it comes with the special set of challenges.

Running any company is difficult enough but factored in relationships with relatives can complicate the picture dramatically. After all, the ultimate weapon we have in management is to terminate an employee. How dicey can that be when it's one of your siblings that has to go; or a father who won't let go of running the family business when he is well past his prime?

There is no secret formula for success. But in these two columns I discuss different approaches that helped both featured families run a more successful and innovative company and thereby secured its future.

The challenges of innovation in a family business

Harry Selfridge, founder of the iconic Selfridges department store in London, was born in Ripon, Wisconsin. He cut his teeth in the retail market by working for Marshall Field's in Chicago. He even built a mansion on Lake Geneva during those years.

But on a trip to London, he saw an opportunity and broke the mold by creating an American-style department store named after him. It was an immense success.

He brought his son Gordon into the business and gave him major responsibilities in the company. Gordon had innovative ideas and objected to some of his father's business strategies. He learned quickly his ideas were ignored.

There was added drama because his father developed a gambling problem and eventually took up with some very young starlets, to the embarrassment of the family, the board of directors and of course, Gordon himself.

This story is so riveting that PBS did an entire Masterpiece special on it.

Family businesses can be a blessing or a curse to the children of the owners.

So how do succeeding generations drive innovation in a corporation that has been wedded to the past and the genius of the founder?

The April 2015 issue of the Harvard Business Review included an article titled "Leadership Lessons from Great

Family Businesses." In it, the authors point out U.S. family businesses "employ 60 percent of workers and are responsible for 78 percent of new jobs. These are not just mom and pop shops either. In one-third of the S&P 500 companies, family members own a significant share of the equity and can influence key decisions, including the election of the chairman."

Owners who create a business can be brilliant, talented and hard-working entrepreneurs. But they can also be guilty of conformational bias or may also have habits that make them resistant to the ideas of a new generation taking the business in new directions.

So what advice do family owners have for others in their shoes?

Cynthia LaConte, chief executive officer of Milwaukee-based Dohmen Co., said having the opportunity to start her own business under the umbrella of the corporate entity was invaluable. It gave her a chance to test her chops as an entrepreneur on her own terms, outside of the shadow of the family business. It also gave the family and the board a chance to measure performance and leadership capability in a neutral and objective way.

Steve Jacobus of Jacobus Co. discovered the importance of having all family members align around a shared vision and mission statement to ensure everyone is on the same page. He feels it is very helpful to have a board of advisors that can mentor younger family members and give objective review of innovation strategies.

The Boldt Co. took a different approach. Bob DeKoch, the president for the past 18 years, along with Tom Boldt, the CEO, and Oscar Boldt, the chairman, helped grow the Appleton-based company into one of the top construction firms in the country. The family then decided to sell a majority interest of the business to the employees under an approved ESOP plan. According to senior executive Jim Rossmeisel, this dramatic step will motivate employees and ensure the future vitality and growth of the business.

The paramount challenge will always be the succession plan put in place to ensure continued strong leadership at the top. The authors of the Harvard Business Review article strongly recommend the establishment of a professional board made up of a significant number of outside directors.

In choosing successor leadership, any family member under consideration should be assessed for a match in basic competencies and values, much as an outside candidate's capability would be considered relative to the company's goals. It is not healthy to hand company leadership to a family member unless he or she has the character, work habits and entrepreneurial spirit to lead the company.

This might not seem fair to family members, but it has to be remembered that the best interests of shareholders, customers and employees trump the feelings of any one person. It's not fair to that son or daughter to put him or her in a position where the child could ultimately cost the company its existence.

Getting counsel through a board and outside coaches is another important tool for family businesses. These resources act as a buffer between family members, bringing experience and objectivity to decision making.

Who knows, if Harry Selfridge had followed this advice, he might have avoided his fate of standing outside his department store as an elderly gentleman, virtually penniless, observing his creation and remembering the times when he was on top of the world.

Family businesses often struggle to adapt to marketplace changes

What's not to like about running a family business? There's a history of success. The family has been running it and understands the business. And the next generation is ready to step up and take over, so succession planning is a no-brainer. Continuing the success of an established family business sounds easy. But guess what? The facts prove otherwise. According to an article in the Harvard Business Review titled: "Avoid the Traps That Can Destroy Family Businesses," by George Stalk and Henry Foley: "Some 70 percent of family-owned businesses fail or are sold before the second generation gets a chance to take over. Just 10 percent remain active, privately held companies for the third generation to lead. In contrast to publicly owned firms, in which the average

CEO tenure is six years, but many family businesses have the same leaders for 20 or 25 years, and these extended tenures can increase the difficulties of coping with shifts in technology, business models, and consumer behavior. Today family firms in developing markets face new threats from globalization. In many ways, leading a family- owned business has never been harder." We live in an age of innovation and disruptive technology. As a result, changes in the marketplace are happening exponentially.

Therefore, what worked for the grandfather founder of the company has little relevance to what's happening in the marketplace today? Family businesses face a daunting challenge because of the inertia created by habits. We all need habits to survive but they also make it very difficult to change or alter course from what's known and understood. Habits are important to our daily existence. If you had to relearn starting your car every day it would take a whole lot longer to get to the office. But with that said, innovation of any kind arises out of the ability to break habits and discover new ways of doing things. Charles Duhigg, the author of the book *"The Power of Habits,"* makes an interesting comment about companies in general: "Companies aren't families. They are battlefields in a Civil War. "If that's the case then it becomes problematic to survive as a family business which is, after all, run by families."

Historically, family businesses tend to make incremental improvements to products and processes. That's invaluable and explains why many do survive. However, making something better is not the same as innovation. A family company making telephones when smart phones disrupted the industry usually spelled the death knell for the family business. According to Vince Shiely, a partner at Lubar

& Co. with a track record of leading operations in major manufacturing companies, our current Wisconsin business climate has become far more challenging for family businesses. "Over the past three decades, globalization has substantially transformed the southeastern Wisconsin centric manufacturing footprint of our largest local manufacturers, severely impacting a multitude of smaller local family businesses that had built their foundations on supplying these operations," he said. "The resourceful owners found ways to reinvent themselves to survive." Tom Bentley, CEO of Bentley World- Packaging, faced a similar dilemma. His family business started as a general contracting business in 1848. It was responsible for many historic landmarks and churches. But when the construction industry suffered a downturn starting in 2007, he recognized that there needed to be a different future.

For years, he had been testing the market by using Bentley's core competency in construction to do specialty and custom packaging for clients. That business was starting to grow robustly. Tom also had a son who was coming into the business. Was it time for him to take over? He was, after all, a Bentley with all of the genetic "right stuff."

Tom did what most CEOs of family businesses are reluctant to do: he pulled the plug on its historic mission as a construction company and focused on his packaging business. At the same time, he recognized that turning this business over to his son might be premature because of his age. He brought in outside help when he hired Dennis Axelson to serve as the company's president and to mentor

Tom Bentley's son and prepare him for eventual leadership. The transition is proving to be a success. The company's market share has been growing and it is acquiring other packaging companies. It now have added packaging facilities in several other states. Bentley has become a leader in product innovation, introducing new environmentally-friendly wooden shipping and storage crates with stainless steel and nylon inserts that can be reused numerous times. Tom Bentley claims he's innovative by nature. I can buy that. At his core he is an entrepreneur willing to face the brutal facts about the industry and his own family, and recognize those facts also represent an opportunity rather than a dead end. His kind of courage and willingness to take risk is a rare commodity. There's no reason a family business with the resources available to it can't survive through innovation.

CHAPTER 3

THE VALUE OF CRITICISM

It's hard for the average person to embrace the idea that conflict is a positive quality in any organization. On a personal level most of us do not embrace conflict as a way we want to relate to our fellow humans.

But in the world of business healthy debate, conflict and criticism are important and critical to the innovation and creative process. Remember any kind of creativity is always an experiment. Unless it's subject to criticism and pushback any such initiative is doomed to potential failures that were not uncovered as it moves through the pipeline.

In visiting Japanese manufacturing plants in the United States, I was always struck how employees seem to run scared. They always felt they could be doing better. When I asked what drove their mindset considering they had number one market share in their industry they told me it was a firm belief that could do so much better!

Enjoy reading how the product development team at one company employed the pushback of criticism to rethink the car design process.

The value of criticism

Who likes to be criticized?

We don't like getting criticism and most people feel uncomfortable giving it. It takes us back to some usually negative memories from childhood.

But Steve Jobs and Bill Gates were notorious for challenging their associates and criticizing their ideas relentlessly.

Professor and author Roberto Verganti described the value of criticism in driving innovation in the January issue of the Harvard Business Review.

There are two types of innovation. One is incremental innovation that most companies do on a daily basis, trying to improve the products and services they already offer their customer base.

The other kind of innovation is disruptive technology, represented by Apple's new iPhones or the original Microsoft operating system.

Those create a blue ocean where competition does not exist because your company enters a space previously nonexistent. Pagan Kennedy, in his book, "How We Dream Up Things That Change the World," argues that existing management is frequently bound by industrial group think. That means we get stuck in our discipline's intellectual ruts. To break out of it, we need a new and different process.

The problem with disruptive technology is that it's so unusual and so different from our normal thinking patterns. Verganti suggested using criticism to formally challenge these new ideas.

It does not start with asking customers what they would like. Henry Ford famously said that if he had asked customers what they wanted, they would have said, "A faster horse."

Disruptive technology might be hiding below the surface of your workforce at your company. Your employees sometimes have a vision that occurs to them because they are so familiar with what the marketplace currently offers.

One example points to the evolution of a new version of the Alfa Romeo. The brand was legendary and featured as the car Dustin Hoffman drove in "The Graduate." However, the company had suffered from decades of competition with German luxury models.

One member of the Alfa Romeo product team asked other members of the team to think of cars differently. They came to the conclusion that people buy premium cars not just to display their wealth, but for the ability to express their passion for driving.

That was the opposite of owning premium cars with super powerful engines and high maximum speeds.

The team eventually focused on developing a smaller, lightweight engine using carbon fiber and reducing the power to weight ratio. The result was a sports car that was highly responsive to the driver's skill and the ability of the car to respond to him or her.

Within a few weeks of the car's release, the entire first year of production had been booked by consumers.

So what's the process that could be used to incorporate criticism in the development of new products that disrupt the marketplace?

Here are steps you can incorporate in your management practices when you seek disruptive technology:

1. **Start with your staff, not your customers:** Customers cannot be expected to envision a different future as they are like all of us – used to their habits and what the market offers. However, your staff can see changes in the environment from a variety of sources, including the competition, and is developing both conscious and unconscious intuition about new directions or new visions. This drill should be an individual one so team members can't influence each other. This encourages them to dig deeply into their own perceptions. Give them at least a month before the first meeting.

2. **Sparring partners:** Michael Farrell in his book "Collaborative Circles: Friendship Dynamics and Creative Work" points to the fact that many breakthroughs in art and society have come through

pairs that trust each other but can constructively criticize each other. He points to legendary pairs who fed off each other: Steve Jobs and Steve Wozniak; Google's founding partners, Sergey Brin and Larry Page; Bill Gates and Paul Allen, just to name a few. The leader should facilitate the selection of the sparring partners.

3. **Testing the hypothesis with an outside jury:** This is where the rubber meets the road and partners get to receive feedback about the proposed ideas. The outside jury should be composed of a variety of people with different backgrounds, perspectives and personalities. This requires you to bring in people from other industries. Frank Krejci, CEO of Strattec, does this drill with major new initiatives. These juries, or "advisory boards" as he calls them, are not bound by the habits of industrial group think because they're from different disciplines.

Creating a new blue ocean to disruptive technology is a daunting challenge and it cannot be done the way normal decisions on incremental innovation are conducted.

Try this blueprint and you may find the new blue ocean for your company.

CHAPTER 4

HIRING CREATIVE TALENT

It's hard to imagine individuals getting together and producing creative and innovative decisions if they are by nature not hardwired to be creative and innovative. But then how does anyone ascertain whether someone as actually creative or could engage in creative and innovative thinking? There is a way of determining that; and this column outlines techniques and other ideas to ascertain the creative potential of candidates before you hire them.

Tips on hiring people with a creative and innovative mindset

If you want to run a company that drives new revenue from innovation, the source of most new revenues, then you have to hire creative individuals with an innovative mindset.

How do you do that?

Katherine Power, chief executive officer of Clique Media Group, a media and marketing agency, held forth in a recent interview in the New York Times explaining how she attempts to identify innovative hires. Her insights include:

>>If the candidate wrote for XYZ publication, did he produce articles which suggested new ways of getting revenue?

>>She asks the candidates when they go home at night, what would they describe as having had a great day?

>>What have they done to create their own experiences, such as a new blog or initiatives within their prior companies which demonstrated the willingness to try something new and unusual, and what was that?

>>She will even ask them how they saved their company money in a creative fashion.

Here's what some of our local leaders have to say about what they do to look for individuals they consider creative or innovative when they bring on talent:

Cynthia LaConte, CEO of Dohmen, a highly successful life sciences company in the Third Ward, says:

"At Dohmen, we're always looking for people that are inherently curious and can perceive the world in different ways. That's what keeps our business fresh and relevant. But there's a fine line between creativity and chaos. A company is a living system – a collective of individuals that navigate as a unit. So you need to establish whether candidates can connect to your company's purpose. I always ask interview questions that explore whether there's a match to our vision and values. Remember – "Culture eats strategy for breakfast!"'

She's a leader who gets it and that's why her company is going places no other company has gone.

Mike Lovell, former chancellor of University of Wisconsin-Milwaukee and now president of Marquette University, is known for hiring outstanding talent. He says:

"Our best candidates and most frequent hires are those who go beyond having great ideas; they also talk passionately about how they've made their ideas happen elsewhere."

The law firm Husch Blackwell has 1,500 employees (partners and staff) located in 19 cities around the country. Paul Eberle, a successful entrepreneur in his early career, is now a deputy CEO for the firm, which acquired Milwaukee-based Whyte Hirschboeck Dudek last year. Eberle says he looks for "a number of qualities that are expected in everyone we hire: creativity, intelligence, drive and passion, to name a few. The real challenge is to find leaders, problem-solvers, people who own the issue and can take any challenge to a successful resolution – while making everyone on the team better along the way."

Paul Jones has been a successful entrepreneur in his own right leading innovative companies and now is a coach to startups and runs a very successful angel network to finance startups. He has a very interesting take: "For founders – the folks with the big, outside-the-envelope vision – you look for fire in the belly coupled with an ability to explain their vision in a way that not only challenges, but respects the less visionary folks they need to inspire (think investors, employees, customers)."

In Jones' experience "arrogant know-it-alls don't get very far unless they have done it before. For the push-the-envelope innovators...you look for fire in the belly, again, but this time in the context of just knowing they can find and use the available tools to accomplish the vision."

In Texas, they would say avoid hiring those individuals who are: "All hat and no cattle." Avoid slick talkers. Look for prior results.

Clearly, there's no simple one-size-fits-all formula.

My suggestion is that you deliberately build in questions that challenge the candidate to describe and document their previous creative and innovative accomplishments in both their business and personal lives.

CHAPTER 5

WHAT TO DO WHEN YOUR COMPANY'S EXISTENCE IS THREATENED?

We live in a world of disruptive technology. There is hardly an industry or segment of the economy that isn't under some threat from new technology and new ways of doing business to the detriment of your company matter how long it's been in existence. History is filled with the number of companies that were not able to react to the demands of a threat from the marketplace.

There's no formula for what to do but there are the examples of others who experienced incredible threats to their very existence.

There's probably not one reader of this book who has not been to a Starbucks. But did you know that in 2008 it was on the brink of insolvency? The stock had dropped to eight dollars a share as fast food providers McDonald's and Wendy's started rolling out premium competitive coffee.

Wall Street analysts did not give Starbucks much of a chance to survive.

Its retired founder Howard Schultz came back from enjoying that experience to fire the incumbent CEO and take over the reins of the company once again. The rest is history. Had you bought several thousand shares of Starbucks in 2008 you would never have to work another day in your life.

Starbucks CEO saves his company

In 2008, we almost lost our opportunity to enjoy Starbucks coffee and the ambience of its stores. The stock had plunged by 65 percent, and same-store sales had dropped dramatically. Wall Street analysts were predicting its demise because major fast food chains such as McDonald's were introducing premium coffee in thousands of stores. McDonald's concluded that coffee was becoming commoditized, and they sensed blood in the water. Howard Schultz, the poor kid from Brooklyn who founded Starbucks, decided to come out of retirement to save this iconic American coffee chain that had become known throughout the world. His motivation was written in his own words: "There are moments in our lives when we summon the courage to make choices that go against reason, against common sense and the wise counsel of people we trust. But we lean forward nonetheless because, despite all risk and rational argument, we believe that the path we are choosing is the right and the best thing to do. We refuse to be bystanders, even if we do not know exactly where our actions will lead. This is the kind of passionate conviction that sparks romances, wins battles and drives people to pursue dreams others wouldn't dare. Belief in ourselves and what is right catapults us over hurdles, and our lives unfold." But passionate conviction and all the good intentions to survive in the world will not succeed without a game plan. So here's what we all can learn from the great turnaround of Starbucks, why it is with us today and did not become another Kodak that ended up on the ash heap of history.

Lessons learned:

1. Start with the brutal facts. What's happening in your industry, with your sales and with your competitors? Everyone on your team needs to know that information and understand what it means to your brand and your company. The tendency to believe that everything will get better is ingrained in all of us. Having the courage to face the facts and accept them is difficult.

2. Embrace uncertainty. This requires real humility. The book Embracing Uncertainty, co-authored by Bob DeKoch, president of the Boldt Company, said, "Those who are absolutely certain of their places in life are the most resistant to change. Every teacher, coach and manager has encountered students, players and employees like these; they are unteachable, uncoachable and unmanageable. They share a core belief in their infallibility; they know all the answers." It is critical that real learners, "readily

admit their lack of understanding." It took a lot of humility for someone like Howard Schultz to admit not only to his employees, but to his customers worldwide that he didn't know the answers. He refused to make predictions of success to the analysts on Wall Street who grilled him about his game plan. He said he didn't have one, but they would unveil it eventually. The stock dropped even more.

3. Ask why you are in business. You would think that Starbucks would have figured that out, right? I often ask business leaders to explain to me in simple terms "What does your business do?" What is your competitive advantage? I often get a lot of gobbledygook. Starbucks was determined "to become the undisputed coffee authority in the world." That's not ambiguous. It's clear and measurable. To deliver on that brand promise was going to take a lot of hard work.

"Infuse innovation practices into the culture."

4. Devise an innovation agenda. Schultz called it a game plan and agenda for "transformation." He probably shied away from the word innovation because Starbucks was such a known brand. But the first thing they did was roll out a new brew that has become one of the greatest sellers in Starbucks' history: Pike Place Roast. It was a powerful catalyst and symbol of their transformation. It offered aroma, freshness, and a little theater so that shareholders had proof that Starbucks was reclaiming its coffee

authority. That new brew enabled them to fight off the competitive attack and re-establish their position as the "undisputed coffee authority."

5. Symbols count. On a Tuesday afternoon in February of 2008 all 7,100 Starbucks stores throughout the United States closed their doors, locked out customers and took a financial hit that ran into the millions. Why? Because fast growth had its consequences. Shultz realized that the quality of what made the Starbucks name strong and invincible – the perfect cup of espresso – was not consistently being delivered at each store. Across the nation, green-aproned baristas watched a short film by their coffee experts who taught them the basics of making the perfect cup of Starbucks espresso coffee. Think about it. The world learned that Starbucks was training its own employees how to make a good cup of coffee. Talk about humility! While Wall St. was yelling "sell," employees were learning how to create the Starbucks experience.

6. Infuse innovation practices into the culture. If you make it through your current crisis, nothing guarantees that you will not be right back where you started in a couple of years. Starbucks began to look for opportunities to extend their brand and expertise to new products that complement coffee. Some ideas included: tea, cold beverages, and horror of horrors, instant coffee. Just last month Starbucks announced it is rolling out a refresher drink to go head-to-head with Red Bull. It's a fully carbonated drink that is high in antioxidants and

uses roasted green coffee. They made a commitment to be innovative with the product they introduce in the market to retain their competitive advantage. Doing the right thing has its consequences … if we had purchased $100,000 of Starbucks stock in early 2008, we would now be sitting on $500,000 of very valuable Starbucks stock. That could buy a lifetime of Starbucks coffee for us!

CHAPTER 6

DESIGNING YOUR WAY TO SUCCESS.

Steve Jobs famously claimed that it was great design made Apple products so unique and popular with the consumers who purchase them. He obsessed on every single detail of every Apple product that ever came out. He applied that same sort of thinking to the design of Apple stores.

He is not alone. Here are a couple examples of companies who learn to apply great design to their products with positive effect.

Reevaluate your core process
"An optimist expects his dreams to come true;
a pessimist expects his nightmares to."

-J.P. Lawrence

Do these problems sound familiar? You are finding yourself in a commodity business with rapidly decreasing margins.

Once the leader in your industry, you now have competition coming out of the woodwork.

Welcome to some of the challenges that Brooks Stevens Inc. faced in the last few years. Brooks Stevens is an iconic brand launched in Milwaukee during the last century. It set the tone and provided leadership for industrial design of consumer products. Just think about some of the examples that Brooks Stevens gave the world: the Hiawatha train, the Oscar Meyer Wienermobile, the Excalibur car, and the first hybrid car in the 1970s.

Brooks Stevens built a solid business serving customers by providing innovative engineering and design solutions. But they were really up against it in 2010. The problem was that the manufacturing sector in the United States was cratering. On top of that, Brooks Stevens was digesting serious problems due to an unfortunately timed merger.

How did they figure out how to survive? Instead of focusing on developing the latest brilliant product, they looked at the process they used to do business and serve customers. They had to think of better ways of engaging their customers and attracting new customers in a difficult market.

Corporations are like people. They develop habits. Those habits prevent them from seeing unique and different solutions to production problems. In fact, companies frequently are too close to a problem causing them to write off potential solutions.

However, Brooks Stevens knew that when it came into a difficult situation it should come without blinders and bring a fresh perspective learned from their experience with multiple industries. It had developed a core skill that allowed them to break down boundaries and create innovative solutions for clients.

So when they faced the challenging 2010 market, they took that core skill set and fine-tuned their approach to how they defined a market opportunity built around helping manufacturers solve problems that they could not solve on their own.

"Innovation is not always about the latest new iPad or light bulb. It can also be about improving the process"

For example, Sauer-Danfoss came to Brooks to develop a new series of joysticks used to operate machinery.

Brooks created a multi-continental design research study that identified surprising regional differences in use from an ergonomic and an interfacing perspective. They visited different regions for research because Sauer Danfoss had an assumption that people viewed technology differently. For example, Houston used simpler joysticks with little or no buttons on the joystick. Houston also had a lot of Hispanic workers, many of whom had smaller hands. This was important to incorporate into the ergonomics. Meanwhile, Europe's joystick was very advanced with many buttons and complex scenarios of use. So they attached a camera into the cab to film people while they worked. The result revealed three different types of operators that used the joystick in unique ways.

In a nutshell, a multi-continental design research study showed that there were different types of operators that used the joystick differently from an ergonomic and an interfacing perspective. These discoveries guided exploration, and several drawings and clay models were designed. Six concepts were selected and created into models for hands on validation research along this line, "Now we get it!"

During BSI's concept exploration stage, their team created many clay ergonomic models with sketch supports that went through many iterations and reviews. They collaborated with Sauer Danfoss and narrowed it down to six concepts to be tested through validation research.

Validation models were molded, and urethane castings with finger function switches were installed. Next they went back into the field to evaluate the designs to determine how the end users interacted with the new concepts.

They even filmed the operators. But this time they had the workers watch themselves in the video so they could witness their new behaviors with the various new concept models. They went deep to validate these models: allowing the operators to handle the concept joysticks right next to their current ones for comparison. For further validation, they held a workshop at Sauer-Danfoss to rate concepts on brand language and manufacturing.

That feedback was incorporated into refined concepts, ready for final ergonomic evaluation and BSI engineering solutions. Brooks assisted I mechanical design for manufacturing and assembly, production design and support.

Sauer Danfoss launched the JS7000 series of joysticks at the 2011 ConExpo in Vegas, where a team from Brooks was able to see the results of their in-depth collaboration. The new family of joysticks was displayed, creating a lot of very positive buzz.

The Cheetah Joystick gives operators improved comfort, ease of control and more configurations. The strength of the product came from understanding the end-users and translating their needs into design solutions.

Remember, innovation is not always about the latest new iPad or light bulb. It can also be avout improving the process of identifying customers' needs and solving them in unique ways.

What does this mean for your business? Look at your processes and see if you can improve those first before you expend major capital dollars on a whole new product or service. It could open up an exciting new opportunity for you!

Designing your way to success

On the campaign trail, we hear Donald Trump telling Americans that we have to stop sending our jobs to China. But if you run a company and suddenly Chinese products have dramatically undercut your pricing, that is a game changer, and you'd be tempted to manufacture in China.

Richard Bemis, chairman of the board for Sheboygan Falls-based Bemis Manufacturing Co., faced this when one of his largest retail customers decided to switch all its toilet seats to a Chinese supplier.

Richard had made trips to China several years earlier to try and understand the competition. He discovered that the Chinese "all in" cost of an employee was less than $1.25 per hour. No time-and-a-half or double time; no health or retirement benefits. They had very few environmental regulations, allowing solvent-based lacquer to be vented into the atmosphere. Conditions were less than safe for the workers, subjecting them to molding resin being made in a garage-like environment.

It became apparent that trying to beat the Chinese on pricing was going to be difficult. But studying the enemy is exactly what generals will tell you is the first step to winning a war.

The strategy, developed by the Bemis sales and marketing team, was to win the war by offering features and benefits that could be protected and that appealed to the toilet seat buyers.

When a random panel of homeowners was asked about their least favorite cleaning tasks in the home, cleaning the toilet was right up there. So, Bemis came up with a seat that can be easily removed from the toilet bowl to make cleaning easier.

Another common complaint was that the toilet seat became loose over time. The STA-TITE Fastening System was introduced to ensure that the seat never loosens. A Whisper·Close hinge was also developed to prevent seats from slamming down. All of these features were patent protected, separating Bemis seats from the non-innovative Chinese look-alikes.

Finally, Bemis significantly increased automation to its assembly lines with new robotic technology. Bemis can now match the Chinese dollar for dollar on their labor costs.

American business leaders could learn from all of this. Bemis is one of the few remaining American manufacturers that makes toilet seats with American workers. To keep jobs and innovation in America, Bemis followed many steps to win the design revolution.

Here are some lessons:

1. **Build a design capability into your manufacturing operation.** Bring designers into the process early to work with engineers to evolve products. Designers are trained to study consumer behavior, thus improving the customer experience in using those products.
2. **Talk to your customers.** Video record them, listen to them and see what new insights you can develop that will give you a competitive advantage. One of the best ideas is to create a "customer journey map" to fully understand the use of your products from their standpoint.

3. **Use prototypes to explore possible solutions to reduce the cost of innovation.** The MIT Media Lab calls this: "Demo or Die." It recognizes that active prototyping can transform an idea into something truly valuable while keeping costs down. Testing through 3D printing is a dream for prototyping.

4. **Tolerate failure.** A design-driven culture recognizes that it's rare to get something right the first time. GE requires teams to try new iterations and then keep pivoting from what they learn.

This is what successful entrepreneurs do when they start companies.

So, here's your homework assignment: The next time you use a private or public bathroom, study the various toilet seat designs and celebrate the fact that the Chinese could not compete with Bemis' innovative design.

And by the way, that large retail customer that switched to Chinese toilet seats is back to selling Bemis toilet seats.

CHAPTER 7

VOICE OF THE CUSTOMER TECHNIQUES

Innovation at any company begins with understanding the problems and challenges their customers face. There are multiple ways to achieve a full understanding of their needs and to uncover unmet needs.

Here is an example of a business leader who found a way to ascertain the needed insights from his customer base.

Understand the problems your customers face

We have all heard the old refrain: "You can't sell ice cream to Eskimos."

Don't tell Todd DeMonte, because he currently sells dehumidifiers in the arid state of New Mexico to solve greenhouse operators' mold problems growing medicinal marijuana plants.

The company he heads, Therma-Stor LLC, has grown under his leadership to become the largest manufacturer of dehumidifiers for both the business and consumer markets in all of North America.

Make no mistake about it, humidity is a big problem in our life, whether it's in our own homes or for those that operate greenhouses or industrial plants. The Therma-Stor team prides itself on asking customers to try its units and make up their own minds about the quality of the offering.

What does DeMonte credit for his company's success? He points to his experience at a Mercedes dealership in the 1990s. Mercedes was under pressure to compete against Lexus, so it drove its costs down but sacrificed quality, to the detriment of the brand.

As a result, DeMonte believes delivering quality to customers is paramount.

His team adheres to the philosophy that customers have challenging problems, but they don't know what the product solutions would be. A horse and buggy owner would never think to ask for the invention of a car.

DeMonte's team feels it is in the "translation business." His employees listen carefully to a variety of sources about Therma-Stor products, from customers to sales reps to people using competitors' products.

They spend their time understanding the problems those customers face and then translate those problems into opportunities their equipment could solve.

Take the marijuana example. In the indoor facilities that grow legal cannabis, it's necessary to control the lights. When the lights are on, humidity levels can easily be maintained. However, when the lights go off, humidity levels rise, creating serious problems such as powdery mildew, spider mites and a whole host of other things that will ruin the harvest.

Anyone in business is flooded with feedback from customers and the market, so the question always becomes: what can our team do about it?

DeMonte historically segmented the company's various product ideas and evenly distributed investment across their various brands. He said he got that idea by trying to treat his kids equally.

Unfortunately, the family makes a lousy metaphor for a successful business. Because we love our kids, we don't fire them!

So instead, Therma-Stor developed a product innovation process that speeds up customer response through various gates to evaluate products. It begins with an analysis of their core competencies, as well as the potential for sales of the product, before anybody engineers or manufactures anything.

We all hear about "The Lean Startup" methodology by Eric Ries, but that applies primarily to software development. Jeff Bezos throws money at his software engineers to innovate. That's not so easily replicated in the mechanical engineering world, where sometimes it's hard to get ahold of raw materials or parts from the supply chain to test a product.

As a result, Therma-Stor can compress the testing process and that, in turn, allows it to focus on those projects it knows will create the most value.

That process has accounted for the tremendous growth of the company to become the leader in segments focused on efficiency, capacity or size.

Therma-Stor's team delivers the most efficient dehumidifiers in the world.

DeMonte hires most of his engineers from the Madison area, where his plant is located. Many are University of Wisconsin graduates. This proves that "Made in the USA" is still a viable option.

We do not have to figure out how to sell ice cream to Eskimos to achieve the kind of results Todd's company has achieved. It starts with a keen, careful listening process, and then turning customers' problems into solutions that delight them. As proof, most of its growth comes by word-of-mouth, and Therma- Stor tracks that by ZIP code.

Innovation begins with careful listening and interpreting the needs of the customer.

CHAPTER 8

CALCULATED RISKS

Everyone in business knows that it's all about taking risks. Those who take risks can be successfully rewarded. But how much risk is too much risk?

It is been argued that really successful business leaders actually reduce risk by facing problems head-on and looking for potential solutions. One such CEO is Frank Krejci CEO of the highly successful company StraTEC. Read how he deals with taking "calculated risks".

STRATTEC CEO learned from running struggling furniture company

How likely it is that a local graduate of a New Berlin high school would end up leading a global company that excels in innovation?

Frank Krejci is the CEO of STRATTEC Security Corp., a global company that designs and manufactures access control products for the automotive industry and other markets. If you own an American car, you're likely using STRATTEC's technology to gain access to your car.

Krejci was a student at New Berlin High School when his wrestling coach asked him if he considered going to Yale for college. Krejci didin't know where Yale was. He ended up wrestling at Yale and then went on to Harvard Business School, where they taught business thinking instead of structured equations.

He learned to be innovative when he took on the role of an entrepreneur trying to turn around a struggling furniture company in Ixonia. He delat with the challenges of keeping the company going. The market for American manufactured furniture was being eroded by foreign competition, their factory burned down and the economy for furniture cratered with the great recession in 2008.

Innovative leadership is not an inherited trait; it is often learned by necessity. It's obvious in meeting with Krejci that he gets excited about the products STRATTEC is bringing to market. STRATTEC ships its products worldwide and last year had sales of $348 million.

There are multiple lessons Krejci took away from running a struggling furniture company. These are some of the practices that have become part of STRATTEC's innovative culture:

>> Vision: It has to be aspirational so everyone associated with the organization knows precisely what they're trying to accomplish. It has to be revisited continually.

Previously, the focus of the company was on automotive access control products. Through their planning process, his management team suggested changing it to just access control products, thus dramatically expanding their thinking about markets for the company's innovative products.

>> Board of advisors: STRATTEC created a board of advisors made up of diverse leaders from the company for each business unit. The board acts as a brain trust to evaluate strategies and new product ideas identified by the management group. They bring different perspective to the innovation process while they themselves learn to think more strategically.

>>Partnerships: After partnering with two privately held companies to establish a global footprint, Krejci is continuing to look for new growth partners. STRATTEC knows its core competency and so it is always looking for organizations that can bring other skills to the table. For example, it invested in a small company that can identify fingerprints for secure entry. This is going to be growth market in the years to come, so why reinvent the wheel when STRATTEC could identify a partner with which ir could work?

>> Reducing risk: The Company doesn't rely on a projection to manage risk. For example, weathermen predict the chance of rain as a percentage. Instead, STRATTEC relies

on a range of projections. Management collectively uses its experience and knowledge to assess the difficulty or ease of reaching minimally acceptable outcomes, and decides accordingly.

>> Urgency: To drive change, there needs to be broad involvement. Then the laws of physics kick in. A body in motion tends to stay in motion.

>> Fun: A sense of fun comes with being creative. Humor is part of the culture, as well as taking time to celebrate the victories.

If you get the opportunity to run your own shop, do it and become an entrepreneur. It's the greatest training on the planet of someday running a worldwide innovative company. If that opportunity doesn't come along, then feel free to visit BizStarts, as we're working with entrepreneurs every day and they could use a mentor. Both of you will learn and you'll be the better for the experience!

CHAPTER 9

STRATEGIC PLANNING AND GOAL SETTING

Americans invented TV and created the technology to bring it to market. Today Japan is the dominant player in not only making TVs but all of their ancillary products. What happened?

How could we be such an innovative leader and yet fail to close the deal by becoming the dominant manufacture of TVs and related products.

So much has to do with the way we traditionally plan and American companies. We develop targets and then pursue those with relentless commitment measuring as we go.

The problem is the world is changing too fast for that traditional planning process to work anymore.

Credit American statistician Dr. Edwards Deming with creating breakthrough thinking when it comes to innovation and creativity. Unfortunately this great American statistician taught this to the Japanese in post-World War II. As a result Japanese auto companies are the leading sellers of cars in the United States.

The key is to be flexibility in planning welcoming and encouraging new approaches immediately without waiting to the end of a lengthy strategic planning process. The Japanese call it *Kaizen* a.k.a. never-ending improvement.

In this column I discuss how companies continually reinvent themselves and pursue new directions in the planning process to ensure growth and survival:

Set goals to drive innovation in your company

Samsung started as a trader of fruit, vegetables and fish that transformed itself into a leading player in construction, shipbuilding, financial services, electronics and consumer appliances. It is now building the largest ship ever made. The chairman of the Samsung Group, Lee Kun-Hee, told his employees with tongue in cheek: "Change everything, except your wife and children." According to The Wall Street Journal, he met with his senior management team in 1993 and gave them the challenge to change just about everything in the company. Kun-Hee's strategy has succeeded as Samsung has ridden the waves of technology leadership to become the world's largest electronics producer, with 200 subsidiaries and \$269 billion in revenues for 2013. It ranks only second to Apple, and even ahead of Google, as the most innovative company in the world. Because of the rate of technological change, your company has probably had to react just to stay competitive. Is it possible to get ahead of the curve? If innovation requires change, how do you manage it? More importantly, where do you begin?

Let's look at a local success story. Stephen Ziegler was an entrepreneur in his own right, having started an accounting firm and scaled to a real success story. InPro, a Muskego-based company that makes interior and exterior architectural building products for health care, hospitality and educational facilities, was struggling financially. Limping along with revenues of just more than $10 million, the sale price was right, so Ziegler decided to buy the company and see if he could make a go of it. Today, it is one of Wisconsin's fastest growing companies, with revenues of more than $100 million and revenue growth of 8 to 9 percent every year. InPro continues to add plant capacity and employees. What happened to turn it around? Ziegler asked this question: If you own a home, you know that every year there are certain projects you need to do to maintain it or improve it. What should you do? Wouldn't you develop a game plan that identified what needed to be done? Wouldn't you then budget for those changes? That is precisely the basic game plan he installed at InPro. Every year, the company developed a list of critical goals and action plans necessary to accomplish those stated goals. Most importantly, they developed a transparent, widely shared tracking system so that everybody could see who's accountable for what.

The Japanese developed a planning process called Hoshin planning. Roughly translated that means following the shining path. Too many companies develop strategic plans that just sit on a shelf. Ziegler makes sure that the game plan is a living document shared continuously with all the employees. They can identify the initiatives they are working on. It could be called a goals progress report. As a result, the entire organization is driven to accomplish things and not be obsessed with trying to earn 20 percent ROI and other profi t metrics, which distract them from accomplishing the kind of quality initiatives necessary to succeed.

W. Edwards Deming, the great American statistician who taught the Japanese how to manage after World War II, would take pride in seeing the accomplishments of InPro. Deming's philosophy was driven by the notion that corporations succeed when employees are valued and trusted and involved in the process of growing the company.

The chief operating officer at InPro, Glenn Kennedy, is a student of Deming. Statistically measuring quality and reaching out to employees to accomplish those goals may not seem very "sexy." But it is the blocking and tackling that makes a great company, and Kennedy understands that.

Improving the quality of processes is clearly a form of innovation and creativity, and those kinds of initiatives find their way into the annual goals progress report.

Ziegler has created a culture in which employees feel empowered to make suggestions and help drive the planning goals every year. He firmly believes that most employees want to contribute and do not need to be spied on or disciplined into performing.

For example, Matt Bennett, the vice president of product development and technical services, drives innovation in the products by listening intently to sales representatives and customers. That is backed up by providing prototypes made from the latest 3D design software to the customer for feedback. When a customer sees the prototype, it becomes very easy to communicate their needs and to come up with the optimal solution. Bennett is also open to learning new ideas that enhance productivity in everything from new materials to delivery systems that can dramatically improve the customer experience.

Ziegler has even developed a program to recognize an outstanding leader of the month. It rewards those employees who are willing to attack problems, find efficiencies or take risk to implement change. They can be nominated by fellow employees or even nominate themselves because they have the right stuff to make changes and follow through.

The reward for the outstanding leader is the use of a company-owned Hummer for a month. The company also has a gainsharing program to encourage teamwork and share the financial success with employees.

There's no magic bullet to innovation and no one right way to do it. But one thing is absolutely certain: having a visible game plan visited on a continuous basis and visible to all employees, while having the willingness to listen to them and then publicly acknowledge their contributions, is fundamentally critical to the innovation and creativity process.

Ziegler can look back with pride at the risk he took because he had a philosophy and a view of how employees could contribute that he was able to implement. If you implement a visible annual goals progress report, you will end up with a company that consistently drives innovation and creativity in everything it does.

SECTION 5

TIPS FOR PERSONAL CREATIVITY AND BUILDING A BUSINESS CREATIVE CULTURE

"An optimist expects his dreams to come true; a pessimist expects his nightmares to"

JP Lawrence

The leader of any organization is responsible for the culture of the company. If you've learned anything from this book you've learned that you do not need to be born the next Steve Jobs to lead a successful company that values creativity and drives innovation.

This section is dedicated to giving you a laundry list of tips you can employ to ensure that creativity is hardwired into your organization.

Again there's no magic bullet but when in doubt or when you get stuck you can turn to the section and look for the tip that would help you.

If you're a golfer and you get a golf magazine you know that every magazine has tips from the pros about how to do a certain shot. This section compiles those kinds of tips.

Identify your problem and here's a suggested solution you can try.

Tip 1: COSTLY MISTAKES: How can we avoid major mistakes or hiccups when we rollout a new initiative, product, or service?

Every creative initiative has an inherent risk of failure. The question is how to reduce the percent of failure?

Annie Duke started her career with a doctorate degree in cognitive psychology. She took a leave of absence from her fellowship at the University of Pennsylvania got married and moved to a small town in Montana. There were not a lot of jobs for cognitive psychologists in her town so she ended up looking for sources of money. That led her to follow her brother's path and to test her skills in the world of poker in Las Vegas.

Was she crazy? Well she ended up winning the World Series of poker and earned more than $6 million in various poker tournaments. This led her to write a book filled with advice on how to play a winning hand. It's called: *Thinking in Bets* by Annie Duke

Her suggestion on avoiding tragedies is to do hardwire in two questions to ask before rolling out a new initiative:

1. If we look back two years from now and this initiative was successful, what did we do right?
2. If we look back two years from now and we have a disaster on our hands, what will we say we did wrong?

Engaging the team and that kind of conversation opens up new areas worth exploring that could lead to enhancing or changing the rollout. It will stimulate creativity enforcement team members to think differently about any given problem.

2. NEW REVENUES: How do we insure a steady stream of new ideas products or services?

One of the most popular and new approaches occurring in corporate America is dedicated staff to a new innovation center

Here's an example of one company that has done this very successfully

Snap-On Tools is a leading global innovator, manufacturer and marketer of tools, diagnostics and equipment solutions for professional users.

In May 2009 it opened its Innovation Works facility in Kenosha Wisconsin

The CEO challenged the new product development leader to create a process that would improve the success rate of new products and increase the velocity of identifying the rate of new products and winning ideas.

The stated goals of the Innovation Works was to create a unique facility that allowed Snap-On Tools to provide their associates with the critical resource needed to further accelerate Snap-On's global innovation.

The 15,000 square-foot facility was designed to support a vibrant user modeling facility.

It contains several defined areas each specifically designed user interaction:

1. A state-of-the-art service garage
2. A prototyping room
3. A 3D modeling facility
4. Display an application room
5. Customer observation room,
6. Innovation library and training room

A small staff of 4 to 5 dedicated individuals who are experts in ethnographic research to help define market needs and that includes conducting customer focus groups, field consulting; invitations to customers to come to the home office innovation center and be interviewed; listening sessions with professional tool users leading to data driven customer research

The dedicated staff included industrial designers to sketch concepts and further revise those concepts based upon continual customer feedback at every step of the innovation. The dedicated staff included industrial designers to sketch concepts and further revise those concepts based upon continual customer feedback at every step of the innovation.

Tip 3: STUCK? If we get stuck either personally or in a corporate setting what are some quick fixes to get us to think differently and bring new perspectives to the problem were trying to solve?

Professor Mihaly Csikszentmihalyi in his book *Creativity* suggests activities that stimulate the subconscious creative process and those can include walking, showering, swimming, driving, gardening, or even carpentry. He suggests alternating between periods of this relaxation i.e. doing nothing or taking on demanding activities such as rock-climbing skiing or whatever get you away from your normal habits.

In his opinion there is no single approach that works for everyone. Individual you have to find out what works best for you. I'm a swimmer. I keep a set of post its at the end of my swim lane and record ideas that come to me with a pencil having learned that ink runs. When the swim is finished I have a whole new perspective and approach to the problems I'm struggling with.

Steve Jobs was famous for going for long walks with his team members or even by himself. Who can argue with his success?

Bryan Mattimore in his book: *99% Inspiration* suggests "creative dreaming". We know enough about REM sleep that it is a total playground for weird and unusual imagination. Put a small Dictaphone or some post-its next to your bed and when you wake up during the night or in the morning see what your brain tells you it's been thinking and then record it.

Sleep is clearly an important part of the creative process that occurs primarily in the right brain as that's where the main source of creativity resides.

So sleep your way to creativity!

TIP 4: FAILURE: It can be a source of creativity

Almost every great entrepreneur grew their startup by using failure as an opportunity to learn, pivot, and heading a new direction that leads to success.

Ray Kroc could not make McDonald's a successful profitable company until he realized that he was not just focused on making hamburgers for profit; but the real money was in making money by owning the real estate and leasing land to franchisees for serious profits.

Apple Computer and Steve Jobs experienced multiple failures in the market when Apple III failed because Steve Jobs did not allow the installation of a fan; or the initial iPhone 4 struggled because it had antenna problems.

Here are multiple examples and what you can do to leverage what you learn to use failure as a springboard to success.

In the world of entrepreneurship it calls on the founders to "pivot" in a new direction from when they started a company.

There can be no innovation without failure

We have all heard the saying that the word for crisis is the same as opportunity in Chinese.

For most of us mortals a stumble or failure is an opportunity to go to a bar and put down a shot and a beer.

Let's examine how others have handled adversity.

We all follow product innovation at Apple Computer Inc. Why? We have no choice. They keep hitting home runs through their product innovation.

They have revolutionized computer retail stores, music, mobile phones and now tablets. Nobody would question that Steve Jobs and company know how to innovate to the delight of customers.

But what the press doesn't talk about very often is the failures. Why? Let's just call it the media preference for American success stories.

Consider the following failures by Apple:

- Apple III failed in the 1980s because Steve Jobs refused to allow the installation of a fan, and as a result those computers overheated.
- The Macintosh computer was underpowered because Steve Jobs overruled the designers who wanted more capacity.
- iPhone 4 had antenna problems and other iPhones overheated to the point of physical danger to consumers.
- Apple Mobile Me service, according to Fortune magazine, got panned on launch.

Good grief! If Steve Jobs can stumble so often, what happens to us lesser mortals?

Here's a little secret and you can pick this up and repeat it daily as the heartaches come: "You cannot create or improve products without making many mistakes." There can be no innovation without failure.

Ask Scott Haag, president and CEO of the successful Moore Oil Co., a Milwaukee distributor of oil and petroleum products. One of his target industries got hit with a new EPA mandate requiring all trucks to achieve cleaner emissions by implementing new technology known as catalytic reduction systems.

Scott saw an opportunity to add to Moore Oil's product offerings and began distributing an additive needed for the catalytic reduction systems to effectively clean fuel exhaust to the point we could actually risk breathing the stuff coming out of the exhaust pipe. It will generate new and unanticipated revenues for Moore Oil.

Think about other Wisconsin entrepreneurs who experienced major challenges that would discourage any optimist.

- Michael Cudahy shared his experience with his new central EKG machine. It failed in its first demonstration to a prospective Illinois hospital customer. He persisted, fixed his machine and went on to grow a great company, eventually selling out to GE Medical years later.
- Harry Quadracci told me his first printing press that he ordered from a company in England, with innovative new technology, turned out to be a nightmare. He survived that to grow one of the largest printing companies in the world.
- George Dalton said he came up with a business plan for what eventually became Fiserv in his late 50s. The bank he was working for at the time thought it was a terrible idea. Lucky George didn't give up.

So how do you address the reality of failure?

1. Start with advice from the great Dr. Edwards Deming: "drive fear out of your workplace." If your employees perceive that their new ideas and new approaches to business will get them into trouble,

they will not try to be creative but spend more time worrying about the blame game.

2. Do a "learning history" every time there's a failure. This is not an exercise in pointing fingers. Rather it is an attempt to learn what happened and determine how improvements could be made. Nobody can learn to play piano or golf well unless they're willing to look at their mistakes and improve their performance. Thomas Edison, after 1,000 tries at finding a filament for the electric light bulb, said he never had a failure. He, "had 1,000 experiments."

3. Persistence. There is a great book entitled "99% Inspiration" by Bryan Mattimore. He makes the point that creativity requires a willingness to stick with it and not give up easily. Most people are not geniuses but get to innovation through hard work.

Remember, everyone in your company must realize that survival depends on innovation and not playing it safe. In fact, the highest risk is continuing the same thing over and over again expecting a different result.

As a nation, Americans have always been great experimenters. It comes with our immigrant heritage. Let's face it, our continent was discovered by Christopher Columbus who was delusional enough to think differently and claim the world was actually round. He convinced the king and queen of Spain to make a risky venture investment in his new enterprise. Now there's an entrepreneur!

TIP 5: Disruption in Your Industry: turning it to the positive

At a major conference for the auto industry Mary Barr, the CEO of General Motors, indicated that: "the auto industry is going to see more disruption in in the next 5 to 10 years that it has experienced in decades."

Peter Peckarsky, currently the president of Commercial Fleet Capital has been in the auto business for a long time (38 years) and has seen it all. He pointed out that innovations in electric cars and self-driving cars will disrupt entire professions.

"It will affect not only be the suppliers to the auto industry, but insurance companies, lawyers, auto supply stores, gas stations etc. An entire industry has been dependent upon the gasoline fired traditional automobile.

America has always been about cars and this will be revolutionary.

The baby boomer generation is still in love with the automobile; however their children are moving into cities with mass transit where owning a car it is not a necessity; as it is in the suburbs. When you look at the cost of parking and insurance plus car payments –gas and repairs –owning a car is more costly then Uber. The millennial's are effectively being chauffeured for less than the cost of owning a car.

The electric car also fits their concern about the environment and they will buy to cars that drive themselves; so it's hard to find any business that won't be impacted some way. All of the major medium truck manufactures are starting to produce electric trucks and on the commercial side of the car and truck business companies will move fast if there's a cost savings along with reduced greenhouse gas emissions."

To succeed in driving new revenues in business it is critical to offer new products and services. Some of those are incremental in nature. Many however will shake the foundations of a given sector of the economy. But how do we do that?

It requires a culture dedicated to looking at the world from a different angle. We are all biased because of our upbringing and our perception of the world. This is particularly true in business when most people don't want to rock the boat and offend their fellow employees.

We are all creatures of habit and people get suspicious of somebody trying to change the world as we know it especially in business.

Who wants to be told they're out of line or look like the outlier?

Therefore it's critical that everybody in any as is organization understand the importance of looking at the world and your products and services from a different angle.

Here's the prescription for some steps you can take to make that a reality.

Breakthroughs require disruptions

Are you willing to challenge conventional thinking? It takes courage, and it's not easy. In his book *"Disruption,"* Jean-Marie Dru, co-founder and chairman of a Paris-based global advertising agency with offices in 27 countries, gave examples of challenging conventional thinking:

»»It was conventional thinking to consider computers as being reserved for specialists. But Apple questioned that assumption.

»»It was conventional thinking that women should grow old gracefully. But Olay beauty products challenged that assumption every day.

Dru argues that disruption is about finding the strategic idea that overturns conventions in the marketplace and that makes it possible to reach a new vision or give new substance to an existing vision. Disruption is all about displacing limits. It is a three-step process that can be turned into a discipline:

1. Systematically identify the conventions. It's not as easy as it sounds. Our habits prevent us from identifying existing conventions.
2. Identify the problem with the convention that creates an opportunity.
3. Envision a new way of solving or removing a limitation.

Mario and Cathy Costantini decided to locate the headquarters and manufacturing plant of their now nationally famous business, La Lune Collection, in the Riverwest neighborhood of Milwaukee. They met with police officials and found that everyone warned them that crime in the area depressed real estate prices and made it difficult to recruit talented employees. Most of the petty crimes were caused by juveniles who had nothing to do. They challenged conventional thinking by founding the Holton Youth Center, which provided an outlet for young people. Their manufacturing plant is now highly successful, and is one of the reasons that Alterra decided to locate its headquarters and plant only a few blocks away. So how do you ensure that your organization systematically identifies conventional thinking and is willing to creatively look for alternatives? Josh Linkner, in his book *"Disciplined Dreaming,"* suggests a test you can administer. Take this to your team and have them answer each statement: strongly disagree, disagree, neutral, agree or strongly agree.

1. Before beginning a project that requires creativity, we always understand clearly what we're trying to accomplish.
2. We are comfortable sharing our opinions and taking risks at work.
3. We have many sources of inspiration at our disposal and rarely run out of sources of creativity.
4. My colleagues have many breakthrough ideas, and we regularly challenge and question the status quo.
5. We regularly use warm-up exercises to prepare to unleash the best in creative thinking.

6. Our brainstorming sessions are frequent, fun, focused and productive.

7. We have in place a system for sorting out the best ideas from the not so good ones.

8. In our company creativity is for everyone, not just something those "art" people do.

9. When working on new ideas, we leave our normal surroundings and find a physical environment that enables our creativity.

10. When my team works together to develop new ideas, we use many different and powerful tools to uncover our best thinking.

11. Our company has a system for measuring ideas and creativity.

12. Creativity is valued, nurtured and rewarded in our organization.

13. We are willing to challenge conventional thinking. We rarely accept things as they are.

14. We have vivid imaginations and often come up with wacky ideas.

15. Once we have a good idea, we usually test it before bringing it to the world.

16. We feel comfortable taking risks and contributing our most innovative ideas with no fear of embarrassment or retribution.

17. We regularly use metaphors and analogies.

18. We generate good ideas, and there's always a clear next step for putting them into action.

If you do not score high with lots of "strongly agree" answers, you have a lot of work to do in the world of innovation and creativity. If you don't do it now, your competitors will do it for you, and the result will not be pretty. Mario's home country was Argentina. When he was a young child, his father applied for a telephone. It took forever because the government was in charge of the allocation of phones. When he came to America, his father asked AT&T for a phone, and within one day they had a new phone system in place. Why? The private market rewards creativity, innovation and delivery of needed services. Your bottom line: "An optimist expects his dreams to come true; a pessimist expects his nightmares to." It is time to start gathering your organization and collectively answering these questions. Find out whether you really do have a culture and organization geared to innovation and creativity!

Tip 6: WHEN TRAGEDY STRIKES: Turning it to an opportunity to grow

Life is much like a roulette wheel. We cannot bulletproof ourselves from all of the potential tragedies that inevitably happen such as when we get fired; loses a spouse; experience a major medical trauma that changes how we function; or are we experience any of the typical horrors that go on every day across America such as ugly car accidents, tornadoes; fire damage etc.

The cynic says that:" life is a bitch, and then we die".

One does not have to be that cynical to know that life comes with its inevitable tragedies and when they strike we will experience grief, anger, and sometimes end up depressed. Even retirement can prove problematic when a high percentage of men die within two years of retirement.

But if we are willing to pick up the pieces and make the kind of adjustments in our personal life that potentially could give us new creative purposes in life. Someone who loses a job can embark on a different kind of career that open avenues never before on their radar.

One of my most dramatic lessons came from Skip Wilson. As a young man he sustained a water ski accident that left him paralyzed for life from the waist down. That's enough to do anyone in. Instead he picked up the pieces and decided that his medical condition would not limit his opportunities in life. He became a national speaker which included appearances at the life insurance industry Million Dollar Round Table annual conference. He went on to qualify and achieve gold-medal status in the Special Olympics. He also married.

He proves that no matter how difficult the challenges that life throws at us we can pick up the pieces and find new purpose and new direction to our lives.

If you learn anything from this book is that applying the lessons of creative and innovative thinking you can turn lemons into lemonade. So often the difference between happy people and unhappy people is that happy people take on the heartbreaks of life and turn them to the positive. It comes with being a human being.

So what are you waiting and this book and the tools it recommends can be your roadmap changing your life, your corporation and the journey all of us take through the roller coaster of life.

I'm your number one fan if you're willing to take up the challenge.

TIP 7 Creativity starts with curiosity both personally and in all organizations

The brain is hardwired to think in a structured logical way. Current science on the brain suggests that occurs in the left hemisphere. The right hemisphere is the normal source creativity. Ray Bradberry said that thinking is of creativity because it's self-conscious. Creativity is spontaneous, but it's also process

In the book Nicola Tesla: Imagination and the Man Who Invented the 20th Century, the author Sean Patrick points out that is critical to expose ourselves to and abundance of ideas, facts, art, and stories that in turn bring your imagination to life.

Therefore creativity begins with curiosity and in your personal life you should take every opportunity to indulge yourself in the wonders of the universe. The author argues that the more material you're exposed to in this world more grist you have for your imagination. Tesla fully immersed himself in the world of electricity. He read hundreds of books. He conducted thousands of experiments and took copious notes. The more varied your knowledge and experiences are the more likely you are to be able to create new associations and fresh ideas.

Your mind has an incredible ability to cross pollinate-that is to connect desperate things to solve problems in unique ways when vision new creations. Einstein attributed many of us physics breakthroughs to his violin breaks which he believed helped him connect ideas in a very different way.

The beginning of genius is always curiosity. Expand your interests in life peak. Seek out new interesting experiences no matter how mundane or inconsequential they might seem to others. Read books, watch documentaries and discuss your ideas with others. No subject, no matter how specialized or esoteric, is off-limits. You never know where your imagination will find pieces of the puzzle."

Your curiosity will lead to more creativity and more imagination in the personal challenges you face in your life.

This same process is that work in a company that can and should create a creative culture by emphasizing things that stimulate the imagination.

Peter Drucker famously declared that in today's business world, because of the degree of disruption due to rapid innovation, businesses must hire and retain "knowledge workers". These are employees who put a great value in developing their intellectual acumen and challenging themselves to learn continually and contribute to the well-being of the corporate entity that employs them.

It should come as no great surprise for anyone that's had children or grandchildren or nieces or nephews to observe that curiosity is an innate capability that they need to survive. They learn to crawl than to walk and to speak; all pretty complex activities and they do it without prompting; without bribes and without punishment.

It's the ability to be curious about our universe that is responsible for the survival of the species. Charles Darwin made clear that its adaptability that accounts for our ability to navigate the challenges of the universe.

I learned this lesson quickly when I transitioned from the law practice into becoming a CEO of a major financial institution that needed turnaround leadership.

There was no way I could do it on my own as my background was not business but law. I had no choice but to turn to the employees and ask for their help. But in many ways they were the problem because the company had significant challenges because of a lack of leadership and a lack of creative approach to solving market challenges.

Of course I could hire new people and I did. But the world of financial services was changing so fast that even the new hires had to develop the ability to think creatively to drive the kind of innovation we needed to grow in a tough environment.

I took Peter Drucker to heart and did create a learning organization. Our management team would meet monthly and dedicated a good part of the meeting to discussion of assigned reading from articles in the Harvard Business Review, or books that were relevant to our industry.

I required vice presidents to circulate relevant state-of-the-art reading material to their staffs and do likewise at their meetings.

As a business leader it is critical that you create a creative culture by encouraging "curiosity".

We are hardwired to be curious and look for creative solutions to our problems since we were just babies.

Unfortunately as the great Dr. Edwards Deming pointed out, schools and then places of employment managed to beat out the natural curiosity and all of us. In the pursuit of grades or satisfying performance reviews we learn not to take risks or think differently about the world we find ourselves in daily.

The job of a business leader is to restore the natural curiosity of its employees by creating a culture that encourages curiosity and exploration of new and different approaches to the challenges of any organization. This is so important that the Harvard Business Review featured curiosity on its cover and offered multiple articles explaining its importance.

Prof. Francesca Gino wrote an article entitled: *The Business Case for Curiosity*, October 2018 HBR in which he identified some dramatic statistics about how corporations view curiosity.

After surveying 3000 employees from a wide range of firms and industries only about 24% reported feeling curious in their jobs on a regular basis and about 70% said they face barriers to asking more questions at work".

What so difficult to grasp is the fact that most current research suggests that organizations who put a premium on curiosity by and large produce greater creativity and solutions in solving organizational problems. He also pointed out that greater curiosity has the byproduct of reducing conflict between employees because they get more curious about learning from each other.

What is particularly disheartening is that in a survey conducted a 520 chief learning officer's and chief development officer's he found they shy away from encouraging curiosity because they believe the company would find it harder to manage people allowed to explore their own creative interests. So while they claim they want creativity and their cultures they frequently reject creative ideas when actually presented with them. Those leaders would avoid conflict in favor of smooth management.

Henry Ford stuck with the black Model T and that gave rise to General Motors and other competing car companies. He should have valued curiosity more.

In one survey he did of over 250 people Prof. Gino found that the level of curiosity declined significantly the longer the employees worked. They were all under pressure to complete their work quickly had little time to ask questions.

So here is what I suggest aided by some ideas from Prof. Gino:

1. Hire curious employees and test for it in the hiring process by asking them to identify creative solutions they have faced in previous positions?

2. Create a learning culture by exercising "humility" that means being a leader who firmly believes that they don't know the answers. That never was a problem for me because I came from the law profession and I really didn't know the answers! But it is counterintuitive to what people feel; they're supposed to know the answers so be prepared for some skepticism.

3. encourage employees to ask the question why; and at every opportunity to share their experiences from outside the organization or workshops they attend to see what they can contribute to solving organizational problems.

Remember all of us are hardwired to be creative so open your organization to curiosity. Creative solutions leverage the natural instincts in all of us. That could not only produce a better bottom line for your company; no guarantees but it will create a culture where people feel more valued and are given the opportunity to impact the growth of an organization and that reinforces the inner capabilities we share as fellow humans.

SECTION 6

CONCLUSION

"It's never too late to be what you might have been"

George Elliott

We enter this world as very creative little creatures. No young baby needs to be taught to use toys; learn to crawl and even try to master the complex activity known as speech. For a young child it takes a lot of creative energy, experimentation and ultimately execution.

Yet they do it naturally driven by the human instinct to survive by controlling our environment. That's what anthropology tells us.

What happened to us that we don't grow up as creative and as innovative as we were when we were young?

The great American statistician Dr. Edwards Deming opioned that the system beats out of us our natural curiosity and desire to learn. Schools require memorization and tests.

Nothing wrong with that but there's little emphasis put on the creative process.

When we join the world of work we find most corporations have inbred bureaucracies that protect long-standing habits in a culture that punishes anyone who "rocks the boat".

The journey of transforming myself into a creative individual was thrust on me by life's emergencies and challenges. Life forced me to learn the creative process and practice it. As a result I'm not only stayed alive but grew as a person but contributed monumentally to the fabric and community in which I live as a father; friend; corporate leader; government official; early-stage investor and founder of an organization that helps entrepreneurs succeed in starting businesses.

I have learned that one of the greatest joys we can have in life is to experience the true process of being creative and using our God-given talents to help improve not only our lives but the lives of people around us.

As you start your own journey you will experience the joy of becoming creative. It probably has already happened to you along the way. And current science suggests that this is psychologically important to us as humans. The University of Chicago Professor Mihaly Csikszentmihalyi in his book *Optimal Experience* described the creative process is causing the psychological state called "Flow". Human beings experience mood enhancement and the joy of accomplishment when engaged in the creative process.

If you are a business leader you can use those talents to free up creativity and innovation in the people employed by the corporations you help lead.

From a management perspective it will require you to give up the long-held belief by most of us the paradigm "that the leader knows best". Most people view a leader as "weak" if they claim they don't know the answers.

But the honest leader let's his followers know he does not know all the answers and invites them to participate in the creative process; thus building a culture that can quickly respond with true creativity and innovation to the ongoing challenges to survival. There may be skepticism at first but in the long run people will step up to the plate and participate in the way they would not have otherwise.

The most important part about creativity is to recognize it's a lifelong capability that will serve you well into old age. Historically the prevailing thought was that as we age we lose brain cells and our ability to be creative. New scientific evidence and studies suggest that in fact it is possible for anyone of any age to increase their mental capacity by the exercise of creative thinking and taking on new challenges.

Rest assure that you will live a more enjoyable productive and satisfying life as you incorporate the creative process into your daily living and your professional life as well.

You can now begin that journey and experience the joy of becoming a truly creative person that drives innovation in your life but in the lives of those around you.

BIBLIOGRAPHY

Jonah Berger, 2016, *Invisible Influence*, Simon & Schuster

Gene D Cohen MD PhD., 2000, *The Creativity Age*. Avon Books, NY

Clayton Christiansen, 2003, *The Innovator's Dilemma*, Harvard Business School Press

Csikszentmihalyi Mihaly, 1996. *Creativity*. HarperCollins NY.

Csikszentmihalyi Mihaly, 1998. *Optimal Experience*, Cambridge University Press, London

Michael Dalton, 2010, *Simplifying Innovation,* Flywheel Defect Publishing, Division of Guided Innovation Group LLC,

Robert DeKoch and Clampitt Robert. 2001. *Embracing Uncertainty*, M.E. Sharpe NY

W. Edwards Deming, 1986, Out Of the Crisis, Massachusetts Institute of Technology

Charles Duhigg, 2012, *The Power of Habit, Random House*

Annie Duke, 2018, *Thinking in Bets,* Penguin Random House Inc.

Barry Feig, 1993, *The New Products Workshop*, McGraw-Hill Inc.

Rowan Gibson, 2015, *The 4 Lenses of Innovation,* John Wiley & Sons

Malcolm Gladwell, 2008, *Outliers*, Little Brown and Company

Malcolm Gladwell, 2005, *Blink*, Little Brown and Company

Jonathan Kao, 1996, *Jamming, The Art and Discipline of Business Creativity*, HarperCollins

Scott Kaufman & Carolyn Gregoire, 2016, *Wired to Create*, Random House

Braden Kelley, 2010, *Stoking your Innovation Bonfire,* John Wiley & Sons

Tom Kelly and David Kelly, 2013, *Creative Confidence*, Crown Business a division of Random House LLC

Pagan Kennedy, 2016, IVENTology, Houghton Mifflin publishing

Jake Knapp, 2016, *Sprint*, Simon & Schuster

Chan Kim and Renee Mauborgne, 2005, Blue *Ocean Strategy*, Harvard Business School Press, Boston MA

Vijay Kumar, 2013, *101 Design Methods*, John Wiley & Sons Inc. Hoboken NJ

Walter Isaacson, 2014, The Innovators, Simon & Schuster

Walter Isaacson, 2013, *Steve Jobs*, Simon & Schuster

Jonah Lehrer, 2009, *How We Decide,* Mariner Press Boston. New York

Jonah Lehrer, 2012, *Imagine How Creativity Works*, Cannongate Books Ltd

Dan Lyons, 2016, *Disrupted*, Hachette Books Group,

Luma Institute, 2012, *Innovating for People,* Luma Institute

Jack Matson, 1996, *Innovate or Die*, Paradigm Press Ltd. Royal Oak Michigan

Bryan Mattimore, 1993, *99% Inspiration,* AMACON, a division Of the American Management Association

Leonard Mlodinow, 2009, *The Drunkards Walk, How Randomness Rules Our Lives*, Vintage Books

Paul Ormerod, 2005, *Why Most Things Fail*. John Wiley & Sons, New York

Dana Oliver, 2015, *Mantra Design: Innovate, Buy, or Die.* Self –Published

Gerard Puchio PhD, Marie Mance, MS, Laura Barbero Switalski. MS, Paul Realli, MS, *Creativity Rising*, ICSCPRESS

Gerard Puchio PhD, Mary Murdoch, Marie Mance, 2007 *Creative Leadership,* Sage Publishing Inc.

Printed in the United States
By Bookmasters